ETIQUETTE AND GOOD MANNERS

Sarah Maclean is the daughter of a diplomat and spent much of her childhood abroad before returning to England to take an honours degree in English at Oxford University. Under her real name of Marie Louise Bruce she has written a full-length biography of Anne Boleyn which was recently published and has earned high praise. She is hard at work on another Tudor biography.

She lives in an Oxfordshire village with her husband and three children.

ETIQUETTE AND GOOD MANNERS

SARAH MACLEAN

REVISED EDITION

PAN BOOKS LTD : LONDON

First published 1962 as
The Pan Book of Etiquette and Good Manners
by Pan Books Ltd, 33 Tothill Street,
London SW1

ISBN 0 330 23778 0

2nd Printing 1962
3rd Printing 1963
4th Printing 1967
5th (Revised and Re-set) Printing 1973

Printed and bound in England by
Hazell Watson & Viney Ltd
Aylesbury, Bucks

CONTENTS

ACKNOWLEDGEMENTS

For the information in this book I owe a large debt of gratitude to many people, too many to mention by name. I should like particularly to thank those young people who gave me their views on etiquette. And I should like to thank representatives of the following: Buckingham Palace; Royal Opera House, Covent Garden; Glyndebourne Festival Opera; St Paul's, Knightsbridge; Ipsden Parish Church; Hyde Park Hotel; Ritz Hotel; Savoy Hotel; Hilton Hotel; Midland Hotel, Manchester; Moss Bros; Annabel's Club; Mirabelle Restaurant; P. J. Green Catering, Thatcham; Church Commissioners; Oxford and Reading Register Offices; Transport and General Workers Union; London Motor Cab Proprietors' Association; Community Relations Commission; Royal Thames Yacht Club; P & O Steam Navigation Company; Spanish National Tourist Office; National Tourist Organization of Greece; Italian State Tourist Department; British Tourist Authority.

ETIQUETTE

SOCIETY HAS changed radically since I first wrote this book. It is an increasingly informal world we live in. Never has society been more causual, more disrespectful of rules, more impatient with old taboos. Authority and age, twin bastions of etiquette, are no longer highly regarded; it is the young who make the scene. And the young are inconoclasts. They sport the uniforms of high-ranking army officers as fancy dress, wear velvet on the beach and cotton on the dance floor and are embarrassed by the word 'class', a term belonging in their opinion to an old-fashioned and crumbling social hierarchy. Society is freer and more fluid than ever before. So why in the permissive 1970s am I bringing out a book on etiquette? What use have we got for it today?

'Etiquette' conjures up visions of Victorian fathers lecturing their daughters' tongue-tied suitors in stuffily panelled libraries, visions of bored and pompous middle-aged women filling their idle lives 'calling' on each other, and all the snobbery of Edwardian days. Etiquette, however, has always existed, even in the most primitive societies. Not only is it part of the ceremony and ritual so strangely necessary to the human species; at its best it forms a code that actually helps people to communicate. It is an accepted familiar habit of behaviour that enables people to be themselves without having to worry about the mechanics of who goes through a door first, when to sit and when to stand and what fork to use. Etiquette can liberate as well as trammel. And never has this been truer than it is today. The rules are still there but their observation, especially among the young, is no longer mandatory. Today they are no longer shackles but good helpful social tools to use or not use at will, and a knowledge of how to use them is still well worth mastering.

CHAPTER 1

GETTING MARRIED

'ALL THE world loves a lover', an etiquette book of the 1920s advised the engaged couple, 'but this does not keep the world from watching closely and criticizing severely any breach of good manners – especially on the part of the engaged girl.' Times have indeed changed. The modern engaged couple go off for weekends together if they wish and it is no longer any business of the world's. Modern society regards people's morals as being their own private concern. Not every family, however, feels the same way – which is the sole remaining reason for most long engagements. Families tend to be less critical of a daughter's behaviour with her fiancé than they are of her behaviour with a mere boy friend. For people without this parental problem, engagements today tend to be short, lasting only as long as is necessary to find somewhere to live and make the preparations for the wedding. For a Saturday afternoon spring wedding in a fashionable London church you may have to book as much as six months ahead.

Couples who are going to get married in a register office often consider it pointless to get engaged at all.

The etiquette the modern engaged couple and their parents observe is simply the best way to avoid hurting the feelings of cousins and aunts and to make relations between the two families as smooth and friendly as possible from the beginning. Traditionally the boy's mother, as soon as she hears the news, is supposed to get in touch with the girl's mother, say how pleased she is and arrange to meet if they haven't already done so.

When an announcement is to be put in the newspapers, it's tactful to tell close friends and relations before it appears, as announcements are for acquaintances only.

CONGRATULATIONS

Relations and friends who can't wish them well in person usually write or send a telegram to either boy or girl, whichever they know. Tradition turns a blind eye on the fact that in the majority of cases it is the girl who brings the man to the point. The convention is to congratulate the man, never the girl. 'I'm so glad, I think John's a super chap,' is roughly what most people say to the girl.

THE ENGAGEMENT RING

Though it's more romantic for the young man to spring the ring as a surprise on his girl friend, most couples prefer to be practical and choose it together, as a ring that suits one hand may not suit another.

At one time it was invariably a precious stone – diamond, ruby, emerald or sapphire – and a young man coy about his finances arranged with the jeweller beforehand to show only those rings within his price range. These days many young couples discuss frankly how much he can afford, and often it is she who decides in favour of a second-hand ring or a large and colourful semi-precious stone, rather than getting an insignificant diamond or spending money badly needed for their future home. Money apart, a turquoise ring, bought on the spur of the moment in a Greek village the night he proposed, may carry far more sentimental value than a diamond ring bought in London three weeks later.

But even the most liberated woman still expects him to write the cheque.

NEWSPAPER ANNOUNCEMENTS

Few people bother to announce their engagement in the newspapers unless they believe they belong to Society with a capital S, when they put an advertisement in the Forthcoming Marriages section of *The Times* or *Telegraph*. For instance:

> MR F. L. NORTH AND MISS M. A. HAWKINS
> The engagement is announced between Frederick Leonard, second son of Major and Mrs R. L. North of Well Lodge, Inkpen, Sussex, and Mary Anne, eldest daughter of Sir John and Lady Hawkins of 13 Wildcroft Street, London SW3.

A BROKEN ENGAGEMENT

If the engagement has been announced in the papers another announcement is usually inserted, like this:

> The marriage arranged between Mr Alan Brown and
> Miss Jennifer Brooks will not take place.

When invitations have already been sent out each guest must be written to and told that the wedding is off. This unpleasant job usually falls to the bride's mother who simply states the fact briefly without going into who broke with whom or why.

If any presents have arrived, the girl or her ex-fiancé, depending on whom they have been sent to, returns them to the giver with a note of thanks.

The girl is also supposed to return the engagement ring and any other valuable presents she may have received from her ex-fiancé. Obviously there is no point in returning anything he can't sell or give to anyone else.

THE WEDDING RING

The couple choose it together and the bridegroom pays for it.

The Traditional White Wedding

This bristles with more problems of organization and more points of etiquette than any other social occasion a woman is likely to meet in her life unless she marries an ambassador or moves in royal circles.

MAKING ARRANGEMENTS WITH CHURCH AND MINISTER

As soon as they have agreed to get married, bride and groom should get in touch with the vicar of the church they have chosen to settle the date and time of the wedding, the reading of the banns and the music at the ceremony.

If they are specially interested in the music the vicar will arrange for them to meet the organist. The vicar or his vestry clerk may also arrange for flowers in the church – when two weddings take place on the same day, flowers are often shared – and the printing of service leaflets.

Just before the wedding, most vicars will go through the prayers and responses with bride and groom and, if they like, supervise a rehearsal in the church.

At a fashionable London church all the fees are usually included in a bill sent out before the wedding. But the vicar will advise on what the fees are and when they should be paid. If a verger's fee is not included, he should be tipped from 50p to £2.10 on the day, depending on the type of wedding.

WHO PAYS ?

Traditionally, most of the onus of paying fell on the bride's parents. Here is the formula.

The bride's parents paid for: engagement and wedding announcements in the Press; wedding invitations; bride's dress and trousseau; wedding-day photographs; printed leaflets for the service; decorations for the church; all hired transport for the bridal party on the wedding day except for the car hired by the groom for himself and his best man – the usual number of hired cars is four; all expenses to do with the reception.

The bridegroom paid for: the banns, or licence; marriage certificate; marriage service fee; verger's fee or tip; music in church; hired car for himself and the best man; bouquets for bride and bridesmaids; buttonholes for bride's mother and his own mother; honeymoon.

The bridesmaids paid for their own dresses.

Obviously this formula only makes sense today where the bride's parents are much better off than the bride. Most people treat it as a basis and compromise according to their means. The modern bride, who is usually earning good money herself, rarely expects her parents to pay for her clothes on top of all the other expenses, and the modern bridegroom usually expects her to pay her whack towards the honeymoon. Even when the bride's parents are well off, many bridegrooms offer to pay for all the hired transport and for the photographs.

But where, as often happens, bride and groom have more spare cash than their parents, they pay all the wedding expenses themselves.

INVITATIONS

The bride and her mother send them out, having first asked the bridegroom's mother for her list of guests, telling her how many are planned for so that she knows how many she can fairly invite. When to send the invitations depends on how big the wedding is to be. The grander the affair, the earlier the invitations are sent out – but for a medium-sized wedding, four to five weeks is usual.

Though the bridegroom's parents naturally expect to be at the wedding it is still customary to send them an invitation.

PRESENTS

If you are asked for your wedding present list how business-like can you be without giving offence? Is it better to risk being called mercenary and list the exact make of china and colour of the bath towels you want, or to risk winding up with a home cluttered with china in a design you can't stand and bath towels that make your walls look anaemic? Most young couples with strong views on furnishings choose the former course, in the belief that their friends will prefer to give them something they really like. To save posting endless carbon copies, bride and groom leave an exact list of the presents they want in a big department store where they are on sale; the shop will then cross off each item as it is bought. But there is one taboo. Though you may prefer a cheque to a conventional present, it is still not tactful to ask unless you are offered the choice. Few people are generous enough to deny themselves the pleasure of giving something that will remind you of them when you use it.

There is no harm in asking for a grand piano if you want it and think there is a chance you may be given one, but it's only kind to your least well-off friends to include things in their price range too. Most people who receive an invitation to a wedding feel they ought to produce a present whether they accept or not.

The bridegroom traditionally gives the bridesmaids a present; this is generally a piece of jewellery, earrings, bracelet or brooch. Bride and groom are also supposed to give each other presents; the bride's present to the groom is often a watch or cuff-links, the groom's to the bride an eternity ring. Though modern brides and bridegrooms are prone to a convenient lapse of memory over this convention, especially if they have paid all the wedding and reception expenses themselves.

Presents from the guests are sent before the wedding – either addressed in her maiden name, to the bride's home, or to the groom's if the giver doesn't know the bride – with a brief message on the enclosed card, such as: 'With love and best wishes for a very happy marriage, from Mary Brown.' It is charitable to send the present as early as possible so that the bride and groom can get their thank-you letters off before departing for their honeymoon. The fairest way is for the bride to thank for those presents that have been sent by her friends and relations, the groom for those that have been sent by his; though needless to say there are some husbands who make her write the lot.

DISPLAYING PRESENTS

They are rarely displayed except when the reception is held in a private house, and then only (for obvious reasons) if the house is exceptionally large. If you are displaying them, what should you do about cheques? The usual procedure is to list 'Cheques From the Following:' and write the names of the givers but not the amounts. Other presents are displayed with their cards attached. If you have been given five toast-racks, the tactful thing to do is to space them out rather than bunching them all together.

WHO CHOOSES WHOM?

The groom chooses the best man and the ushers; the bride chooses the bridesmaids. The best man is usually the groom's best friend, the chief bridesmaid the bride's.

WHAT THE BEST MAN DOES

The bridegroom is generally supposed to be in a high state of nerves on the day, and it's the best man's job to help him through his ordeal and see that he doesn't make any mistakes, that he's on time for the wedding and that he catches his train or plane for the honeymoon without leaving the luggage behind. The best man collects the bridegroom from his home and drives with him to the church; he takes charge of the wedding ring and makes any on-the-spot payments to the vicar or verger, or any last-minute arrangements for the honeymoon the bridegroom may ask him to. The bridegroom should give him a sum of money to cover all expenses.

WHAT THE CHIEF BRIDESMAID DOES

She looks after the bride, making any last-minute adjustments to the bride's dress in the church porch, supervising the other bridesmaids and usually helping the bride to change into her going-away clothes after the reception.

ARRIVING AT THE CHURCH

The most popular time for weddings is the early afternoon.

The ushers should arrive half an hour, the guests about quarter of an hour before the time stated on the invitation card. The bride's mother and the groom's parents usually arrive just a few moments before the ceremony.

It is the ushers' job to ask guests: 'Friend of bride or groom?' and seat them accordingly, bride's friends and relations on the left of the aisle, groom's on the right. The left top pew is reserved for the bride's immediate family, the right top pew for the groom's. Other relations should also be given a seat near the front.

The bridegroom and best man should arrive at the church about twenty minutes before the ceremony and go to the vestry to fix up any last-minute formalities. They then wait for the bride either in the right-hand pew or on two chairs in front. The bridesmaids arrive just before the wedding and wait for the bride in the porch.

The bride and her father arrive on the dot.

THE CEREMONY

The bride walks slowly up the aisle on her father's right arm, followed by the bridesmaids. Brides who are nervous of walking up a long, empty aisle may be preceded by the choir. The bride joins the bridegroom – bridegroom and best man stand up when the bride appears in the porch – in front of the chancel steps and stands on his left. Her father stands behind and to the left of her. The best man stands behind and to the right of the bridegroom. The chief bridesmaid comes forward and takes the bride's bouquet, and gloves if she's wearing them, then goes back to her place. Where the bridesmaids are adults, the chief bridesmaid is one of those in front; where the bridesmaids include children and adults or very young and older children, the smallest ones lead, but one of the adults or older children normally acts as chief bridesmaid, stepping forward from the back of the procession to take the bouquet.

When the minister asks: 'Who giveth this woman to be married to this man?' the bride's father, without speaking, steps forward, takes the bride's right hand and gives it to the minister, who puts it in the right hand of the bridegroom. After the plighting of the troth, the best man steps forward and gives the ring either to the clergyman or to the bridegroom (the clergyman will indicate which). The bridegroom then takes the ring and puts it on the bride's finger. The bride's father and the best man, when they have done their bit, usually remain standing, but they can go and sit down, if they like.

After the ceremony is over, the minister leads the bridal couple into the vestry to sign the register, followed by both sets of parents, the bridesmaids and the best man and, if the vestry is large enough, sometimes an old family friend. The bride signs her maiden name for the last time. The two witnesses are usually one from the bride's and one from the groom's side.

The bride then walks down the aisle on the groom's left arm, followed by the bridesmaids in pairs. If there is an odd number of bridesmaids, the best man may join the procession, otherwise he usually walks round the side of the church and waits in the porch. After the bridesmaids come the bride's mother with the groom's father, and the groom's mother with the bride's father. Everyone then joins in behind, the top pews generally emptying first.

After the photographs have been taken outside the church,

people leave for the reception, the bridal party in the hired
cars first, in this order: bride and groom, bride's parents,
bridegroom's parents, bridesmaids. Though at very lavish
weddings a few hired cars are sometimes laid on for the
guests, they are more often left to follow on as best they can
in their own cars or in taxis. The best man and the ushers
should stay behind to see that no one gets stranded.

THE RECEPTION

This is usually held a few minutes' drive from the church,
traditionally in the bride's parents' house or a marquee on
their lawn at a country wedding. But since few houses are
big enough to accommodate a large party, most people have to
opt instead for reception rooms in a hotel, or the village hall.
A wedding reception lasts on average from two to two and a
half hours. Grand cocktail-party-type food – canapés, *vol-au-
vents*, sandwiches, etc – is laid out on a long buffet table.
At a small wedding guests may be left to help themselves but,
if the room is very crowded, it's obviously better, though more
expensive, to have the food handed round. The traditional
drink at a wedding reception is champagne, but some people
economize by drinking a sparkling white wine and serving
champagne only for the toasts. This is, of course, still pretty
expensive. A popular alternative to having the stuff flowing
all the time is to serve one drink when the guests arrive,
usually sherry, and just serve something sparkling for the toast
drink. A peculiarity of the wedding reception is that no one
is expected to do much in the way of introducing. The best
man or an usher may rescue someone standing all alone, otherwise guests are left to introduce themselves.

MAKING ARRANGEMENTS

The least expensive way to hold a reception is to do most of
the catering yourself with some help from the local bakery,
buy your own drinks and hire someone on the day to help

with cutting up the cake, handing round drinks and washing up. This, of course, is only possible with a small wedding. Alternatively, you can get in a firm of caterers who will make all the arrangements, providing food, cake, drink, flowers, extra china, linen and waiters – or you may arrange with them to provide your own cake and drink. If you hold the reception in a hotel, the hotel will also see to everything for you. The tip in a hotel is often paid at the same time as the bill and is usually ten per cent of the total. If you are hiring a firm of caterers, ask the man with whom you have made the arrangements whom you should tip and how much.

THE RECEIVING LINE

Bride's mother, bride's father, groom's mother, groom's father, bride and bridegroom line up in that order inside the door of the reception room to receive guests. At a large wedding where there is a danger of the doorway becoming a bottle-neck, the guests move quickly along the line, greeting and shaking hands with the parents, kissing the bride and telling her she looks lovely, if they know her well enough, and congratulating the bridegroom. At a small wedding, where there is no one to announce names at the door, it's a good idea to introduce yourself to anyone in the receiving line you don't know: 'I'm Mary Smith. I work in the same office as Belinda.'

THE CAKE

For a big wedding this is usually white and three tiered – the top tier is traditionally supposed to be kept for the christening party of the first child. Bride and groom cut the cake about twenty minutes after all the guests have been received – or appear to cut it. A wedding cake, sticky with fruit and brittle with icing, can be tricky to carve and it is usually cut beforehand to save the bride and groom wrestling with it. The waiters then take the cake away to divide it into slices which are handed round just before the toasts.

TOASTS AND SPEECHES

How many toasts and speeches you have is up to you. The usual number is three. An old friend of the bride's family or the bride's father says a few words about the bride, usually some embarrassing anecdote about her childhood, wishes the young couple happiness and finishes by proposing the toast to the bride and groom. The bridegroom replies, thanking the bride's parents for the reception and the guests for their presents, and proposes a toast to the bridesmaids. The best man replies, saying something complimentary about the bridesmaids and a few words about the bridegroom. Young couples who find this all rather overwhelming sometimes choose to have the first two toasts only, cutting out the best man's speech. Alternatively, they may opt to have no speeches at all, just a simple toast to the bride and groom.

At a large wedding there may be a special toast-master to announce the toasts. At a small wedding this isn't necessary; the best man can simply ask for silence. The important thing to remember if you are asked to make a speech is to keep it light, since the tears of the bride's mother may be very near the surface.

Here are some sample speeches:

Old Friend of Bride's Family

'It is my pleasant duty to propose the toast to the bride and groom. I have known Jane ever since I was asked to be her godfather eighteen years ago. I little thought as she screamed heartily at the font that she would turn into the gorgeous creature she is today. I have known David for a very short time in comparison – a mere two years – but what I have seen of him reassures me that he will make my delightful god-daughter a wonderful husband. Ladies and gentlemen, David and Jane' – here he holds up his glass – 'may they have every happiness and success.'

Bridegroom's Reply

'This is supposed to be the bride's day, but I can assure you it is the most important day in my life, too. Thank you all for your good wishes and for so many lovely presents. I should also like to thank my parents-in-law for this wonderful party. Last but not least, I should like to thank the bridesmaids for performing their task with such grace and charm. Ladies and gentlemen, I give you the toast to the bridesmaids.'

Best Man's Reply

'I know none of you want to listen to a long and tedious series of anecdotes from the best man. So I will simply say on behalf of the bridesmaids, thank you very much for the nice things you have said about them, which I for one heartily agree with.'

TELEGRAMS

People who have received invitations to the wedding and can't come usually send a telegram, such as, 'Have a wonderful marriage. Lots of love. Charlotte.' The telegrams are often read out by the best man after the speeches. Some best men read them out before giving their speech to give themselves courage.

GOING AWAY

Some time after the speeches, bride and groom go to change, the groom often accompanied by the best man and a bottle of champagne, the bride by the chief bridesmaid. Hotels and reception rooms provide special accommodation for this. The bridal couple go back into the reception room briefly before leaving, or someone may pass the rumour round or announce that they're ready to go. Everyone then crowds round the door to speed them on their way.

Guests are expected to leave shortly after the bride and

groom, not before. If the bride's parents post themselves in the doorway, guests say goodbye and thank you, otherwise they simply drift off.

The old-fashioned etiquette of writing a thank-you note to the bride's mother is seldom observed by young people today; though any bride's mother after going to all the trouble and expense that arranging a wedding and reception entails may be glad to know that her guests enjoyed themselves.

THE WEDDING BREAKFAST

An alternative to the early afternoon wedding followed by a reception is a morning wedding followed by either a sit-down or a fork lunch, styled a wedding breakfast. Usual seating arrangements are: bride and groom at the head of the table, bridegroom on the bride's right. On the bridegroom's right, the bride's mother and next to her, the groom's father. On the bride's left sits her father and next to him the groom's mother.

The 'wedding breakfast' can also take place in mid afternoon. At smaller weddings many people prefer to give their guests a substantial meal rather than the more conventional cocktail-party-type titbits.

SCOTTISH WEDDING RECEPTION

This varies in a few details from the conventional English reception. It is the minister who proposes the toast to the bride and groom, and he does this immediately all the guests have passed the receiving line. But propose the toast is all he does at this stage. He simply holds up his glass and says something like: 'The bride and groom.' Bride and groom then cut the cake. The wedding party then usually has a sit-down meal, and the cake is served with the coffee. After this come the speeches: first the minister's – on the same lines as the old friend of the family at an English reception –

then the bridegroom's reply, then the best man's. Dancing follows.

Formal White Wedding Clothes

THE BRIDE

The classic pure white dress with long sleeves is still the prettiest style and the one most often worn for large weddings. At the time of writing, many of the dresses have an Edwardian look and are worn with a hat instead of a veil.

The theme for brides is demure prettiness rather than sophisticated glamour – pale lipstick and not too much eye shadow. Jewellery should be kept to a minimum. The engagement ring is worn on the right hand during the ceremony.

A white bouquet is the most appropriate, but it can be any colour. More important is that its size and shape should flatter the wearer – small, plumpish girls should carry a small slim bouquet that flows down the dress.

BRIDESMAIDS

The bride chooses any colour she likes for their garments, but rarely all-white or they might detract from hers.

When the bridesmaids are paying for their own dresses, the bride usually agrees to something that can be converted into a party dress afterwards or dresses made of some pretty but inexpensive material.

MOTHERS OF BRIDE AND GROOM

They wear dress-and-coat outfits, usually in grey or pastel shades, not black, and a frivolous hat.

GROOM, BEST MAN, USHERS, BRIDE'S FATHER

If the bride is wearing a formal white dress, at large fashionable weddings it is traditional for them to wear morning dress, see page 191, and a white flower in their buttonholes. At most weddings, however, the men simply wear their best suits.

WOMEN GUESTS

Trousers are still only rarely seen on women guests at conventional weddings. Most of the older women wear short dress-and-coat outfits or suits. But for a late afternoon register office marriage followed by a party they tend to wear long dresses. Most young girls wear long dresses regardless of the time of day. Both young and old usually wear hats to a church wedding, if they go to the church.

MEN GUESTS

If the groom, the best man, the ushers and the bride's father are wearing morning dress, they should, conventionally speaking, wear morning dress too, though some of the younger men tend to appear in more original garments, such as frock-coats and white suits.

GOING AWAY CLOTHES

The old rule was that brides changed into a pale-coloured suit, grooms into a lounge suit. The modern bride prefers a trouser-suit, but anything goes today, so long as it looks smart and is comfortable for travelling.

Informal Church Wedding

Some people prefer to get married quietly, without all the fuss and expense of a formal white wedding, and entertain a few friends to lunch or to drinks afterwards. In this case bride and groom get married in the clothes they're going away in – the bride in a suit and a pretty hat, the man in a dark lounge suit. The bride's father still gives her away and there is a best man, but bridesmaids are out of place.

Register Office Marriage

When two people get married in a register office it is usually because they prefer to avoid the fuss of a white wedding; but there is no reason why they shouldn't have a formal reception afterwards, if they wish. In this case they invite only their nearest and dearest to witness the marriage in the register office and ask everyone else just to the reception. As they have no best man or bridesmaids there will be at most two speeches, and bride and groom will get married in their going-away clothes.

But sometimes people who get married in a register office through lack of religious conviction still want all the glamour and romance of a church wedding. Then the bride dresses up in white, the groom in a smart lounge suit, and occasionally even bridesmaids and a best man follow them into the office and stand behind them during the little ceremony. As many guests as can be accommodated pile into the office – it's as well to check on the size of this before issuing invitations.

Dinner Dance Reception

Dancing at a wedding is coming back into vogue among those who can afford to keep the drink flowing for longer than the conventional two hours.

The form is to get married as late as the vicar or register office will allow in the afternoon. Some sort of light snack is then usually served, the toasts are drunk, and the music starts up. Setting up a bar serving spirits usually comes cheaper than serving champagne only all evening. Supper is served at about eight o'clock and the festivities go on until the young couple leave.

Newspaper Announcements

A wedding announcement in a national newspaper is worded like this:

SMITH: BROWN. – August 6th, 1972, at St Blank's Church, Oxford, JOHN BERNARD SMITH, eldest son of Mr and Mrs J. R. SMITH of Oxford,

to SUSAN MARGARET, younger daugher of Dr and
Mrs R. B. BROWN of Elmpond Square, London
SW10.

Or if the wedding was a quiet one in a register office:

SMITH: BROWN. – August 6th, 1972, quietly in
London, JOHN BERNARD SMITH, eldest son of Mr
and Mrs J. R. SMITH of Oxford, to SUSAN MAR-
GARET, younger daughter of Dr and Mrs R. B.
BROWN of Elmpond Square, London SW10.

Some local newspapers which go in for detailed reports of
local weddings will give you a form to fill up to ensure that
all the details are correct.

How to get Married and what it will cost

IN CHURCH (CHURCH OF ENGLAND)

(1) *By Special licence*. With this licence, granted by the
Archbishop of Canterbury, you can get married at any time
and in any specified place, but these licences are only issued in
exceptional circumstances. Applications for a Special Licence
must be made to the Faculty Office, No 1, The Sanctuary,
Westminster, SW1.

(2) *After banns*. When your marriage is to take place after
the publication of banns, the banns must be called (*a*) if you
and your fiancée live in the same parish, in the parish church
of that parish or (*b*) if you live in different parishes, in the
parish church of both parishes. Except in very special circumstances, when banns of matrimony have been published,
the marriage must take place in the church or one of the
churches in which the banns have been published. The banns
must be published on three successive Sundays before you can
get married.

(3) *By bishop's licence*. One of you must have lived for
fifteen days immediately prior to your application in the parish

in the church of which your marriage is to take place (subject to the exception in (4) below). Marriage licences are obtainable from the Diocesan Registry or a Surrogate, and information as to the fee for the licence will be given by the Diocesan Registrar. You can be married on the same day as you get this licence.

(4) *In a Church which is 'usual place of worship' – by licence or banns*. This is an exceptional provision for people who attend and are on the electoral roll of a church outside the parish in which they live, and wish to be married in that church. Banns are then called in the church where the ceremony is to take place as well as in your parish church (or churches).

You can also get married in church according to the rites of the Church of England, if your clergyman agrees, with a superintendent registrar's certificate – though this, in fact, is rarely done.

Banns and licences alike hold good for three months only, and except in the case of a special licence, the marriage must be celebrated between 8 AM and 6 PM.

In the majority of parishes the Church Commissioners' standard table of fees is in force and the basic fees for a church wedding are:

	£	p
Publication of banns	1	5
Certificate of banns		70
Marriage service where Organ not used	4	
Marriage service with organ	8	
Certificate of marriage		50
Special licence	25	

Choir, carpet, bell-ringers, flowers, service leaflets and the organist's fee are extras to be arranged with the vicar. With a professional choir the cost of a big society wedding in one of the fashionable London chruches can be an expensive business.

IN A REGISTER OFFICE

A Superintendent Registrar's certificate is necessary if you wish to get married in a register office. It can be issued with or without a licence.

Without a licence. If you both live in the same registration district you give notice of marriage to the Superintendent Registrar of that district. If you live in different districts you must give notice to the Superintendent Registrar of each district. You must then wait twenty-one clear days before you can be issued with a certificate. You must have lived in the district for the seven days before you give notice.

With a licence. You need give only one notice whether you both live in the same or different districts. But one of you must have lived in the district for the fifteen days before you give notice. You must then wait one clear day – other than a Sunday, Christmas Day or Good Friday – before you can be issued with your certificate and licence. You can then get married any time within three months from the day on which your notice was entered in the notice book.

Whether you get married with or without a licence, the notice can be given by either of you. If you get married without a licence, the fees amount to £3, or £4 if you live in different districts. If you get married with a licence, the fees total £8.

Expenses at Reception

These vary enormously according to the quality of food and drink, how many waiters you have and where you hold your reception. One fashionable London hotel charges £4.25 a head for 100 guests, £4 a head for 200 guests, £3.85 a head for 300 guests – inclusive of food, drink, cake, reception and changing rooms, linen, china, cutlery, waiters, toast-master and flowers. Alternatively, you can pay a basic £1.50 a head for accommodation and buffet, and pay for the other items separately. A tip of ten per cent is usually added on to the account. This is, of course, a lavish do.

A modest party in the village hall can be a very much less expensive affair. With a glass of sherry per guest on arrival, one toast-drink each and a stand-up buffet, it can cost as little as 100p a head for the caterers' fee; or 130p a head for a sit-down buffet.

CHAPTER 2

OTHER MILESTONES IN A WOMAN'S LIFE

Expecting

ONCE UPON A TIME you only whispered the news to your mother and your closest friends and, as soon as ever it began to show, stuck close to your own hearthside knitting tiny garments and dreaming of the patter of little feet. Modesty about pregnancy has gone the way of modesty in general. The main reason today's expectant Mum doesn't always blazon the news abroad for the first two or three months is simply that it is a bore to be treated like a senior citizen by her friends and given the Granny chair at a dinner party when she still feels a gay young thing at heart. Also, she might just miscarry in the first few months. Pregnancy makes no difference to the modern girl's social life. She goes to parties up until the last moment and carries on with her job until it's economically convenient to stop.

In the later months she wears smocks, caftans and dresses in a firm material, not through embarrassment about her condition but for aesthetic reasons; the bulge is basically an ugly shape.

When it Arrives

An announcement of the birth is sent to either a local or national newspaper along these lines: On February 15th, 1973, at St Blank's Hospital, London, to Shirley (née Brooks) and John Hedges, a daughter (Mary Anne).

Close relations and intimate friends usually send flowers and/or telegrams of congratulation – post offices sell special baby greetings forms. Small posies incidentally are more welcome than grand bouquets in wards where space and vases are limited.

Visitors usually bring something useful for the baby – it's considerate to check what other people are bringing; first babies tend to get too many little knitted jackets, third babies too few! Other presents appreciated by new Mums are bottles of fruit squash to help down the masses of water they have to drink and small bottles of toilet water; and chocolates if these were forbidden in their pregnancy diet.

The baby's birth must be registered within forty-two days by mother or father – or when this is not possible by someone present at this birth.

The Christening

Most christenings take place within the first three months for the purely practical reason that an older child may prove a difficult armful. Christenings usually take place in the early afternoon, but some churches have their own rules as to days and times and it's advisable to consult the minister well in advance.

GODPARENTS

The prayer book says that a girl should have two godmothers and one godfather, a boy two godfathers and one godmother. But there is nothing to stop anyone following the royal family's example and giving their child more or fewer godparents of either sex. Godparents are generally chosen from among relatives and close friends and should belong to the same religious denomination as the child's parents, if the baptism service is not to be a mockery. However, all that most godparents these days feel is expected of them is to send the child presents on its birthdays, and a prayer book or bible on its confirmation; if it is confirmed.

Anyone unable to get to the service can become a godparent by proxy.

THE SERVICE

This is all written in the prayer book and is very simple to follow. The minister indicates to the mother and godparents when they should gather round the font, and the godparents read the responses. Usually one of the godmothers stands on the minister's left and gives the child to him to baptize, so she must hold it during the prayer before the prayer book says: 'then the priest shall take the child'. A godmother, the mother or a nanny holds it during the rest of the service. When the minister demands the name of the child, the godmother on the minister's left answers, giving the child's christian names, or all the godparents may answer together.

Where several babies are christened at the same service, the service is the same except that the minister says 'children' instead of 'child'.

What happens if your baby is mixed up with the one before and gets christened Gertrude Pearl instead of your carefully chosen Caroline Anne? This did happen once in the case of twin girls in a pram which was pulled rather than pushed to the church door. But the minister simply switched the names round in the register, and no harm was done.

After the service the father goes to the vestry and enters the baby's name in the register. As there is no fee for a christening, he should put somethng in the church box.

THE CHRISTENING PARTY

Occasionally when a family is particularly eminent – when the child, for instance, is heir to a title – a christening is made an excuse for a grand party and formal invitation cards are sent out. But in general, christenings are very informal affairs to which only relations and a few old family friends are invited, by letter or telephone. A lunch or tea party follows, either sit-down or buffet according to the numbers and space.

It's usual to provide a christening cake – either the top

layer of the parents' wedding cake or a white-iced cake with or without the baby's name on it – and a bottle of champagne in which to drink the baby's health. Otherwise food and drink is on an everyday level. The obvious person to propose the toast is a godfather, but there are rarely any speeches.

CLOTHES AT A CHRISTENING

The men wear lounge suits, the women dresses or suits and pretty hats. The baby wears the family christening robe, if yours is the sort of family that has one, otherwise its best white frock.

PRESENTS

Godparents always, other guests at a christening usually, produce a present. The traditional present is either silver – a mug, bowl or napkin ring – or jewellery – a child's bracelet or necklace. But these days presents tend to be more practical: money to start a post office account, savings certificates, a toy or a baby garment. Where silver is given it is likely to be something the child will be able to use when it is grown up.

Wedding Anniversaries

There is no reason why a couple shouldn't celebrate any anniversary they please, but those most often made an excuse for a party are the Silver (twenty-fifth), the Golden (fiftieth) and the Diamond (sixtieth). The furthest most members of the 'upper classes' usually go is to put an advertisement in the paper, ring up a few relations, order some champagne and a cake with a discreet little plaque and hold an informal family party. But what the 'upper classes' do is no longer the criterion now that everyone feels entitled to do his or her own 'thing'. A great many people feel that twenty-five years or more of marriage should be marked by a grand party.

Here then are the main features of the celebration:

As many as possible of the people who were at the original

wedding are invited. Husband and wife cut the cake together; it has silver decorations for a Silver or Diamond Wedding, golden decorations for a Golden Wedding. The couple's health should be drunk, the toast being proposed by the eldest son or the best man, and the husband should reply. For a very large party formal invitations are sometimes sent – in silver for Silver and Diamond Weddings, in gold for Golden Weddings.

Guests bring a present in keeping with the celebration. For a Silver Wedding, you might, for instance, bring something tied with a silver ribbon.

TELEGRAMS FROM THE QUEEN

If you write to the Queen's assistant private secretary enclosing a copy of the marriage certificate, the Queen will send a telegram of congratulation for a Diamond Wedding anniversary or any wedding anniversary after the sixtieth, at intervals of five years. Thus if you get a telegram from the Queen on your Diamond Wedding, you can get another one on your 65th, 70th and 75th wedding anniversaries.

COMING-OF-AGE PARTY

When a formal birthday dance is given, specially engraved formal invitation cards are sent and a toast is usually proposed, in which case the hero or heroine of the hour should reply. But formal coming-of-age dances are rare even among the dwindling number of girls who have been debutantes. Parents are more likely to give a cocktail party for which they send out ordinary At Home cards, or to treat their offspring and a party of his or her friends to the theatre and dinner afterwards. But where, as so often today, eighteen-year-olds have more money to spend than their parents, they throw the party themselves.

When a Death Occurs

The general feeling these days is that grief is a private thing and ostentatious public display better avoided. Except in remote parts of the country, blinds are no longer pulled down in the house and, instead of each member of the family in turn sitting up with the corpse all night, the dead usually remain at the undertaker's until the funeral.

Funerals tend to be simple and quiet. The custom is growing for the immediate family only to follow the coffin to the graveside, friends attending the service in church or chapel and leaving immediately afterwards.

Men rarely wear morning suits except at the funerals of very eminent persons – usually they wear dark lounge suits and a black tie. Similarly – except at very grand funerals – women wear black only if they happen to have it, otherwise something plain and dark. It is usual to wear a hat, veil or headscarf.

ARRANGEMENTS

The doctor's certificate must be taken to the register office and the death registered before the arrangements for the funeral can be made; the death must be registered within five days. The clergyman, if he's a friend, can be called in to advise on an undertaker. Alternatively, the undertakers – or funeral directors as they prefer to be called – can advise on a church service and get in touch with the clergyman for you. The undertakers will also, if you like, cope with newspaper announcements and, if many people are expected at a large country funeral, arrange for cars to meet the train.

NEWSPAPER ANNOUNCEMENTS

Few people feel like writing to inform anyone except relations and intimate friends when a death occurs. Instead they put an announcement in the local or national newspapers including the time and place of the funeral service so that anyone who wants to may attend. Announcements are on these lines:

> On January 1st, 1972, at — Hospital, John Smith, after a long illness. Service at St Luke's Church, London SW3, on January 8th at 11.30. Cremation at Golders Green, family only. Flowers to (address of undertakers).

Sometimes people request 'No flowers, please', and ask for donations to be sent instead to a charity the deceased was interested in.

FLOWERS

They should be sent to arrive on the morning of the funeral at the address given in the announcement, with the name of the sender and a brief message of sympathy on the attached card – 'In loving memory', 'In deepest sympathy', or whatever your feelings dictate. The name of the deceased preceded by 'The late' is written on the envelope.

LETTERS

It is still etiquette to write a letter of sympathy as soon as you hear of the death. People who feel these letters only prolong the agony can include in the announcement of the death the request, 'No letters, please'.

The bereaved relative should write and thank everyone who has sent flowers and/or a letter of sympathy. A single sentence will do – simply, 'Thank you for your beautiful flowers and kind sympathy'. But sometimes when this would entail a large correspondence printed cards of thanks are sent instead to people who are not intimate friends and relations. Alternatively, acknowledgements may be placed in the newspapers.

> The family of the late Mr David Smith wish to thank all relations and friends for kind expressions of sympathy and beautiful flowers received during their sad bereavement.

But sticklers for old-fashioned etiquette might consider this rather casual.

THE SERVICE

The service can either be held in church, the body being taken afterwards to crematorium or cemetery or, in the case of cremation, the dead can be taken straight to the crematorium and the service held in the crematorium chapel. A few cemeteries also have chapels where a service can be held.

If the dead was not a practising Christian there is no need to have a religious service, although such a barren end is exceedingly rare.

AFTER THE FUNERAL

If there are only a few people at the funeral the custom is for the bereaved relative to invite them back to the house for a drink or a cup of tea to cheer them on their way home.

MOURNING

At the beginning of this century there was an elaborate etiquette and a fixed time of mourning according to degrees of kinship: two years for a husband, one year and nine months' full mourning (mainly black), three months' half mourning (grey, lavender, purple or black and white), diamonds permissible before the end of the first year, gold ornaments not; one year for a parent, six months' full mourning, six months' half mourning, the wearing of diamonds, but not gold, permissible at the end of three months . . . There were rules, too, about when it was correct to enter society again. Anyone who didn't abide by these rules risked social criticism.

These days mourning is purely a matter for the individual and how he or she feels. Few men wear black ties except at the funeral and fewer still wear black armbands. As for women, black and lavenders, once considered mourning colours, are now fashion colours and no longer carry any special significance.

Most people prefer to keep their sorrow to themselves, picking up the threads of normal life as soon as they cheerfully can.

CHAPTER 3

THE HOUSEWIFE

THE NEWLY-MARRIED wife's job begins with furnishing the new home – a task that has become increasingly easy to do well, since shops in recent years have become so much more design conscious. Now they abound with beautifully designed furniture and furnishings. The only object in the house that remains atrociously and almost universally hideous is the fireplace. A well-designed modern fireplace is still very hard to find. But fashions in snobbery have changed and good taste is no longer the sacred cow it was.

For those who care, however, what the upper income groups think, it is worth noting that certain objects are considered by them to be in bad taste. Most despised among these are curtains hung to face the street, gnomes in the garden and mass-produced ornaments on the mantelpiece.

Getting to know the Neighbours in the Country

Kind near-neighbours drop in soon after a newcomer has arrived to offer help with the first day's shopping, a heartening cup of tea, or information on where the best shops are and when the baker's van calls. In a small community neighbours may also invite you to coffee or drinks parties where you can meet more people. What to do if no one drops in or invites you anywhere ? Then it's up to you to make the first move. The old taboo that older residents must make the first approach has gone. And you can always get to know people by joining in communal activities such as the Women's Institute, the Parents–Teachers Association or local amateur societies.

Complaints

This is one of the many cases where good manners are good strategy. Supposing you live in a flat in town and the people next door keep you awake every night. You can thump on the wall and yell at them to be quiet, for goodness' sake! But nine times out of ten you will get far better results if you invite them in to coffee in a friendly way and in due course let it be known that your husband has insomnia and could they try to be a little quieter.

The same applies if you're in the wrong yourself. Your cat spends its spare time rooting up your neighbour's seeds and she sends you a peremptory little note. Go and see her, explain how difficult it is to keep the cat in, but you will do what you can. Probably you will be able to work something out together and good relations will be restored.

Giving a Party

If it's likely to keep other people in the building awake, it's only considerate to forewarn them. There's all the difference in the world between being told two days in advance by the young couple upstairs that they're going to give a birthday party and they hope you'll look in for a drink, and simply waking up one night to find all hell let loose on your ceiling.

And from the hosts' point of view it's well worth a few drinks to keep on friendly terms with other residents and ensure against the party being brought to a wretched end by furious shouts and threats to complain to the landlord.

Borrowing

Few people mind lending the odd bit of tea, sugar or butter to the people in the next flat when they've run out. But they do mind if they are never paid back. Even if they're not hard up for money they may be hard up for shopping time. The only way to deal with the borrower who never pays anything back is never to have any tea, sugar or butter when she asks for it.

When money is borrowed it should always be returned as soon as ever possible.

Television Manners

Treating the television as a background for conversation is one of the grimmest of failures in the social graces. When visitors come the television should be turned off unless they have come expressly to see it or they are close friends who drop in without any warning, when it would be fair to say, 'Do you mind if we just watch the end of this?' then switch off when the programme comes to an end. Otherwise guests may be justified in presuming that their hosts find the television more entertaining than their company. Though this may well be true it's not tactful to let them know!

Manners for Modern Children

Children today are more intelligent and less tiresomely shy than their predecessors but their manners horrify the parents of an older generation. Instead of listening respectfully to grown-ups, they interrupt and monopolize the conversation and generally treat adults as though they don't exist, and there is not much that today's parents, brainwashed by psychological theory, can do about it. The easiest solution until they have learned to let adults get a word in edgeways is to let them say their piece then shoo them all into the garden or another room to play. But in small houses, and with only children, this isn't always possible. So, granted that one's children's standard of manners is going to be pretty basic anyway, what is the most one can expect?

I think they should learn to treat adults as though they do exist, they should say hallo and goodbye and 'Thank you for having me'. They should say please and thank you at the dinner table and call adults Mr and Mrs unless asked to call them by their christian names. They should ring and thank for a birthday or Christmas present if they can't be persuaded to write a thank-you letter. They should not climb on other people's furniture or leave muddy footmarks on clean carpet or linoleum. Ideally, they should not make rude remarks about the food when they go out to a meal or ask for things that haven't been offered, but to teach small children this is hard labour.

Schools

The first problem is to get your child into the school of your choice. For the most popular state schools, as well as the most popular public and private schools, children often have to be put down at birth. That goes for nursery schools also. For help with the selection of a public or private school write to a London scholastic agency stating your price range and any other special requirements, such as the district you'd like the school to be in, and you will be sent free of charge the prospectuses of suitable schools. For parents wishing to select the best possible state school it is possible to visit a school before deciding to move into the catchment area.

If you want to see the headmaster or headmistress, ring up the secretary and ask for an appointment. A recommendation from another parent whose child has been to the school can help a great deal when there's a waiting list for a public or private school. At a state school you can sometimes indicate a preference for a particular class with a particular teacher. You can also ask for brothers and sisters to be separated.

One advantage of the most modern state schools is that a good parent-teacher relationship is encouraged. They will answer your questions about little Matthew's progress, and you can tell them of any special problem at home which is perhaps making Matthew particularly difficult in class. To maintain this happy situation, it is worth remembering that a teacher's classroom is her kingdom; and it is tactful to ask her permission before marching into the room and asking Matthew to show you his books.

Helping them learn to read? It's as well to find out where the teacher stands – some teachers appreciate help at home, others think it interferes with their method.

The Doctor

What to do if you think you need to see a specialist? Whether you want to go privately or on the NHS you must ask for a letter from your GP. The chances are he will give you one – but suppose he refuses, unjustifiably you think, there is an etiquette you can follow. Thank him for his diagnosis but say you still don't feel happy; could you have a second opinion? Then suggest the specialist of your choice. If he still refuses to give you the necessary letter, you can either change your GP or complain to the Executive Medical Council.

There is another complication that can arise in a relationship with one's GP. What do you do in an emergency when you can't get hold of him and your husband, or child perhaps, appears to be at his last gasp? This situation can still unfortunately crop up. You can ring 999, but if the ambulance driver refuses to come without your doctor's authorization, you can always drive the patient straight to hospital yourself – bearing in mind that there are some conditions in which it would be dangerous to move him.

Though GPs may make the occasional mistake, they can also be exceptionally kind. Can you, without embarrassing your doctor, give him a present? Doctors do in fact get quite a number of presents, especially at Christmas time, usually impersonal things such as a bottle of wine or whisky, cigarettes or cigars.

In Hospital

Maddening as it is to watch your nurse after she's removed the thermometer purse her lips and hide your own temperature from you, dismissing your questions with a smilingly vague: 'Nothing to worry about', this is hospital etiquette. The nurses are not supposed to tell patients what's the matter with them. It's up to the doctor to tell you or not, according to whether he feels it would be good for you to know.

Supposing you can never keep him long enough by your bedside to question him? Then your best course is to ask the ward sister. She may tell you herself, especially if she thinks you're worrying about having some dread disease which you haven't in fact got. If she feels it's not her business to tell you, you can ask her to let the doctor know that you'd like to see him.

Alternatively your next of kin can always ask to see the doctor or specialist in charge of your case.

HOSPITAL VISITORS

The person to get hold of on the telephone if you want to visit a patient out of normal visiting hours or to find out how he is, is the ward sister. But only the next of kin or the person standing in for next of kin will be told the details. Anyone else will have to be satisfied with such stock generalizations as: fairly comfortable, passed a good night. This again is hospital etiquette.

PRESENTS

In the public wards few patients give anything to anybody, faced as they are with all the extra expense of being ill. But private patients often feel they would like, on leaving hospital or nursing home, to express their gratitude in some tangible way. If a nurse has been specially kind many people give a bottle of sherry, a box of chocolates, a book token or a couple of theatre tickets. Alternatively one might give a cheque or a large box of chocolates to Sister for all the nurses in a ward.

But there are hospitals where nurses are not allowed to accept presents, and there are also some nurses who are embarrassed by them. In this case, the best thing to do is to give something towards the League of Friends that provides extra comforts for patients and hospital staff.

Patients with private rooms sometimes tip the orderlies.

Shopping

Household shopping can be one of the trials of the early days of marriage. You ask for a pound of steak and while you're wondering if you can fairly say, 'Not that piece,' the butcher has cut you off a slab of something you don't like the look of at all. Too shy to protest, you meekly accept it and at dinner your husband complains it is tough. Shopkeepers expect you to insist on getting what you want, and if you don't, if you find you've been given a bad pineapple for instance, it's perfectly fair to take it back.

Assistants in most shops are increasingly hard to find, especially if you want to buy something in a hurry. But occasionally a sales-woman can be embarrassingly persistent. What should you do when you're trying on a garment and she stands at your elbow continually telling you how nice it looks and leaving you no time to make up your own mind? The best shop assistants don't do this, knowing that if they force you to buy something you're not going to like, the chances are you won't come back to that shop again. But if you meet one who does, tell her firmly and politely that you'd like to be left alone and that you'll come out and tell her when you've made your decision.

It's all too easy to be bullied into buying something that doesn't suit you by remarks like: 'You'll never get anything that fits you better than that, Madam', or: 'That's how they're being worn nowadays', when the thing is plainly two sizes too big.

But there is another side to the picture – the customer who treats an assistant like dirt knowing that she is in no position to answer back. It is not fair to try on everything in the shop and waste some poor assistant's time when you have no intention of buying.

The fair course when one has a complaint to make about a purchase is to seek out the assistant who sold it and complain to her. Only if she can't or won't put things right should one ask to see the manager.

All you have to do is fill in a form and produce a bank reference and usually two business references as well. These could be two local shops that know that your credit is good.

How to open a Bank Account

Simply go into the bank you have chosen and tell one of the cashiers you wish to open an account. He or she will then probably arrange for you to see the manager, and you will be asked for the name and address of someone who can give you a reference. This should be someone who has a bank account – not necessarily at the bank you have chosen – and who has known you for some time.

Customers are entitled to see their bank manager at any convenient time and ask his advice on any matter on which he's competent to give it, what investments to sell out and whether such and such a house is worth buying, for instance. At a big city bank you may have to wait longer than you would at a small provincial branch, but your bank manager will never refuse to see you.

The time you *must* see your branch manager is when you are contemplating overdrawing your account. If you do this you are borrowing the bank's money and it's only courteous to let him know.

You will be shown how to make out a cheque when you open your account. But there is a point of etiquette here. Though from the bank's point of view it is quite correct to make a cheque out to M. L. Smith, it is more polite to make it out to Miss, Mr or Mrs M. L. Smith. Cheques should always be endorsed, when necessary, in the same way as they are made out. If a cheque is made out to you as Mary Smith, you should sign it Mary Smith, not M. L. Smith.

Letters to the bank are addressed to the manager – in spite of the fact that he's very unlikely to read most of them – begin 'Dear Sir' and end 'Yours truly (or faithfully)'. But customers who have met him often, begin 'Dear Mr Smith' and end 'Yours sincerely'.

Help in the House

'Lady Swordstick is pleased to say that the reference of Jane Duster is satisfactory and she would be glad therefore if she would enter her service as housemaid on June 10th as was arranged.' This imperious little note was, according to an old etiquette book, the correct way to engage your staff in 1927. Jane Duster started work at 6.45 in the morning, received a pound a week pay, got one afternoon off a week, and every other Sunday for church.

How times have changed! Old-fashioned servants have virtually disappeared. In their place are the 'helps' whose status is very different from poor little Jane Duster's. And the question these days is not seeing that they do their work satisfactorily so much as treating them well enough so that they stay with you and don't seek more congenial employment elsewhere.

THE DAILY HELP

She is paid by the hour the local rate for the job, which varies considerably. If she doesn't live locally, her fare is usually paid as well.

Unless she is a young girl, it is usual to call her Mrs Blank and she will probably call you Mrs Blank, too.

The Living-in Help

These days she is usually a girl from abroad, obtained either through friends or an agency. In order to get a work permit if her nationality still makes this necessary, you must apply to your nearest Employment Exchange who will give you a form to complete in which you must state the particulars of the employment you are offering, including the wages. These must accord with those paid to British girls doing similar work in the same district. Employment Exchanges will advise on local rates.

Who pays the fare varies. Many employers advance the fare then deduct it from the girl's wages, but pay the money back to her if she stays for a year.

NANNY/MOTHER'S HELP

The chief problem here is to make it clear from the start where her duties end and Mother's begin. Is she to mend the children's clothes as well as doing all the ironing and cooking everyone's lunch? It is important to work out the timetable so that she is not on duty from early morning to late evening without getting a rest in the middle of the day.

Another problem is dinner. Dinner *à trois* puts a strain on all three. A usually acceptable compromise is for everyone to have lunch together and the girl to have high tea with the children.

TIME OFF

The minimum is one full day a week, a fortnight's holiday with pay, and one weekend a month. Evenings off is a bargaining point. But most employers give as much time off as possible in the knowledge that if a girl is not happy in her present job there are plenty of others going. For everyone's sake it is important to make it quite clear from the start what time the girl can call her own.

LAUNDRY AND TELEPHONE

Most employers allow her to send her towels and sheets to the laundry if they use one, but expect her to do her personal washing herself, using their washing machine. Local telephone calls are usually on the house, unless she has a great many. If she had frequent long trunk calls it would be fair to ask her either to pay for them herself or to cut them short in future.

WHAT TO CALL HER

If she comes from abroad and has been in domestic service there, she usually expects to be called by her christian name whatever her age. If she is English, the modern tendency is only to call her by her christian name if she is a young girl and for her to call you Mrs Blank.

FRIENDS

These days most employers would allow her to entertain her friends, including the steady boy friend, in her own room. Some people allow her to entertain her friends in the sitting-room when they go out for the evening. However, before making a concession like this, it is obviously wise to wait and see what the girl and her friends are like.

THE AU PAIR GIRL

All she needs in order to get into the country is a letter from you inviting her to stay in your household as an *au pair* and stating that you will make arrangements for her to learn English in this country. On arrival she will receive a booklet from the Home Office. This says that she should not be expected to do more than about five hours' work a day, in exchange for which she receives her keep and pocket money. She must have one full day off a week, time off for classes and should be treated like a member of the family. This means that she will expect to have dinner and sit with her hosts in the evening unless she prefers not to. Obviously the system is open to wide interpretation and it is advisable for the girl to know as much as possible about the job before she enters the country. She usually pays her own fare over.

THE BABY-SITTER

She expects to do nothing but sit and see that the children come to no harm. Unless she lives next door she will expect to be fetched and returned by car and, if it is to be an all-evening session, she will expect to be left something with which to cook herself a meal. There is usually a local rate for the job.

REFERENCES

When one first engages anyone to help in the house it seems appallingly insulting to cast doubt on her honesty or ability by asking for references. Experience, however, proves that it really is essential to ask for references and most people expect to give them, either written references or the name of a previous employer you can write to or telephone. If it's a girl's first job, the school or college will probably give her a reference. When asking questions of a previous employer, it is as well to remember that the employer will probably be unwilling to say anything derogatory unless asked a question point-blank: Has she any major mental or physical problems? Is she trustworthy? Could I safely leave her in charge of the children?

But there is another side to the coin. Your prospective help may well wonder what sort of employer you are. If you can put her in touch with a previous employee who will tell her the job is lovely, it may well help to clinch the deal.

CHAPTER 4

THE CAREER GIRL

THE FIRST essential for getting ahead in any career is efficiency but, since the success of a firm depends on team work rather than the ability of isolated individuals, an easy and pleasant manner and a capacity for fitting in run a very close second. A pattern that constantly recurs is that where two girls are equally competent one gets passed over and the other gets promotion, the reason being that one has a gauche manner and a prickly personality, while the other is a pleasure to work with.

A naturally prickly personality can be camouflaged by courtesy and consideration for others. But the business world is different from the social world outside; it has its own quirks of etiquette and its own pitfalls. There are many situations in which knowing the form can help to smooth the newcomer's path. It can also help her to land the job in the beginning.

Letter of Application

Writing this letter is writing an advertisement for yourself and how you phrase it and set it out is immensely important – especially if there is a lot of competition for the job.

The golden rule is that it should be easy to read, neatly set out, clearly and precisely expressed and as brief as possible. The letter should be typed unless otherwise stated in the advertisement. Like all business letters, it should have the name and/or status of the person you are writing to and his address either on the top or the bottom left-hand side of the page. Your name should be typed under your signature with Miss or Mrs beside it.

A busy employer has neither the time nor the patience to

wade through pages of irrelevant waffle, so go straight to the point. State (1) for what job you are applying: 'I am applying for the job of assistant advertised in the *Daily Blank*, June 5th.' (2) What qualifications and experience make you suitable for the job (shorthand and typing speed in the case of a secretary, what jobs you have held and how long for, any relevant certificates or diplomas). (3) Why you want the job – this is your opportunity to show originality, personality and a keen interest in the work. Unless asked to state your terms in the advertisement it's not advisable at this stage to mention pay and hours. (4) Your age. (5) When you can come for an interview: 'I could come for an interview any afternoon next week', never, 'Should this application meet with your approval, I shall be glad to place myself at your disposal for an interview at your convenience.' Long-winded and obsequious cliché phrases of this kind will lose you a job for which there is any competition.

If all the information won't fit on one side of a sheet of writing paper, the best plan is to list qualifications and experience with dates on a separate sheet and write a brief covering letter.

'Yours sincerely' is the correct way to end, if you write to a prospective employer by name, 'Yours faithfully' if you begin 'Dear Sir (or Dear Madam)'. Never 'Yours hopefully' or 'Yours in anticipation'!

Gimmicks such as elephantine envelopes addressed in green ink may pay off if you're going into advertising or publicity, but my advice is to steer clear of them in any other business. An employer may think you don't know the correct way to address an envelope or that it should fit the writing paper inside.

The Interview

The first essential is to get there on time. Arriving late is not only rude and inefficient, it makes one flustered too. It's a wise precaution to allow a few minutes for getting lost in a maze of passages, being sent up to the office of the wrong Mr Adams or any of the host of accidents that have a way of happening if you arrive on the dot. Give your name to the receptionist: 'My name's Miss Smith. I have an appointment with Mr Adams', and offer to wait if you're early. You will have to wait a few minutes in any case while your interviewer is told you are there.

Anybody tempted to discuss Mr Adams with another occupant of the waiting room should bear in mind the following cautionary tale: One girl nervous about her approaching interview with the editor of a well-known magazine asked the pleasant-looking man sitting opposite her if the editor was as awful as gossip held him to be. Not until she had related the fruity worst did she discover she was, in fact, talking to the editor!

Probably a secretary will come and collect you, open the office door for you, announce you and close the door behind you. But your interviewer may collect you himself, in which case, he will probably stand aside to let you enter the office first. If your interviewer is a woman, it would be polite to let her go first.

Say good morning or good afternoon to your interviewer, but wait for him to offer to shake hands. The tactful course throughout the interview is to leave the initiative with him, stand until he asks you to sit, don't smoke unless he offers you a cigarette (don't, whatever you do, go into his office smoking – he may regard his office as his castle and take it as a personal insult), wait for him to ask the questions. There is only a limited number he can ask you and you should have been able to foresee them and know roughly what you are going to say beforehand. A question he will almost certainly ask is why you want to leave your present job, and in answering this it's not good policy to run down your employers; he may get the impression you're not likely to be happy anywhere. If you have been out of a job for some time, he will probably want to know the reason.

But there are bad interviewers. What should you do if he appears at a loss for what to ask? Prompt him with something of this kind: 'Would you like me to tell you exactly what work I did in my last job?'

Some interviewers pride themselves on tricky questions such as: 'Tell me about yourself, Miss Smith.' The answer to this one is to do just what he asks. Tell him what your parents did for a living, where you went to school, what your hobbies are, highlighting anything particularly to your credit – that scholarship you won, for instance.

Another tricky question is: 'What can I tell you about the job?' Don't be lulled into thinking this means the job's yours for the asking and your signature on the dotted line and start talking about pay and time off. Stick to asking about the work, using any cues that present themselves to show just why you are the right person for the job. Leave it to him to bring up the question of terms. An employer has to be very desperate to take on someone whose prime reasons for taking a job are the salary and holidays.

If you're unlucky enough to come across the interviewer who deliberately tries to embarrass you by beginning: 'What can I do for you, Miss Smith?' your only possible reply is to throw the ball right back to him: 'You asked me to come and see you about a job, Mr Adams.'

YOUR MANNER AT THE INTERVIEW

This is one of the occasions in life when one has to forget everything anybody ever told one about modesty and blow one's own trumpet. If you say that you don't think you can do the job your interviewer is not likely to think so either. The difficulty here is to give the impression of quiet confidence in your ability rather than cock-sureness, remembering that you are being interviewed not only to find out how able you are but also whether you're likely to get on with the rest of the staff. You will get good marks for pleasant, unaffected manners and a sense of humour, but it's unwise to show this at the expense of the firm's products, as one man discovered when being interviewed for a job in advertising. His crack about the immorality of the advertising game was met by a moment of poker-faced silence followed by a lecture to the effect that the country's economy depended on it.

CLOTHES FOR THE INTERVIEW

Exactly what clothes you wear depends on the kind of job you are after. If it's anything to do with fashion obviously your clothes should be as up to date as possible. The golden rule is: decide what sort of person your prospective employer is looking for, then dress to suit the part. Safe stodgy clothes will probably not land you a job that has anything to do with fashion; on the other hand if you have set your heart on joining Messrs Bloggs & Sons, the oldest and most solidly respectable firm in the City, it would be a mistake to turn up for your interview looking too trendy.

Most firms still like to cultivate an image of efficiency and reliability and the clothes their employees wear can help to create this impression. One point worth remembering: prospective employers over forty hate scruffiness; with them good grooming still wins good marks. They like clean brushed hair, tidy clothes, neat feet, handbags that are tidy inside as well as outside. And most of them still can't stand too much hair on young men.

References

For many jobs references are not necessary. But if you think one is likely to be helpful, you can either ask for a written reference from your old employer when you leave his firm (the head of your school or college if it's your first job) or you can ask if he'd mind if you gave his name as a reference, in which case your new employer can write to him or ring him up. Before giving anyone's name as a reference it's good manners to ask their permission.

A written reference should be handed to you in an unsealed envelope and should say how long you've worked for the firm, what your work was and how well you did it.

Written references are not usually enclosed in a letter of application. They are either produced at an interview or sent afterwards; it's accepted practice to send copies in case the originals might get lost. If a prospective employer insists on being sent the originals, he's in honour bound to let you have them back.

The Newcomer

The first few weeks as a junior in a new job are rather like being a new girl at school, and it's not a good idea to throw your weight around and start off by suggesting a way of revolutionizing the office filing system or asking the boss out to lunch.

On your first day, someone should take you round the offices introducing you to the people you will have to deal with. As for the work, if you don't understand it, the first few weeks are the time to ask and keep on asking. No one expects a newcomer to grasp everything at once and it's far better to ask twice about something in the first week than to make an elementary mistake after you've been with the firm two months. Don't follow the example of the new junior in a magazine office who hid two pages because she was too frightened to ask what should be done with them!

Even though nobody else observes them, the new junior should stick to the office rules, arriving on the dot in the morning and taking no more than the allotted time off for lunch. Taking liberties with the rules is an executive's privilege and anyone who is constantly late, even though her work may be good, is storing up trouble for herself.

GREETINGS

Saying good morning when you come in and goodnight when you leave is part of ordinary good manners. But it's not so easy to know what to do if you are late one morning and find yourself sharing a lift with the directors. Should you start up a bright conversation? Or maintain a remote silence and hope they don't notice you? It's obviously unnecessary to do anything if you haven't met them. If you think they know who you are, my advice is to smile and say good morning and leave them to start any bright conversation.

WHEN YOU ARE UNAVOIDABLY LATE

There are times when you can't help being late, when you cut your finger instead of the bread or something goes wrong with the plumbing. When this happens, the form is either to ring your boss yourself or get someone else to ring him. In the case of illness, if it lasts more than three days most firms ask for a note or certificate from your doctor.

KNOCKING ON DOORS

In a civilized firm nobody knocks on office doors unless they are going to see some important person with whom they normally have very little to do. The only other time it would be good manners to knock is when something may be happening on the other side of the door that you're not supposed to hear. In this case, you can give a warning knock and enter without waiting for a 'Come in'; alternatively, simply stick your head round the door and withdraw if you're obviously interrupting.

But the custom varies from firm to firm. If in yours everyone knocks on everyone else's door, genteel and unnecessary though this is, the most tactful course for a newcomer is to follow suit.

LUNCH WITH A COLLEAGUE

The custom is for each to pay his or her own share.

SECRETARIAL MANNERS

They shouldn't present any difficulty if you use common sense, tact and ordinary courtesy. Obviously no boss wants to be interrupted in the middle of an interview except for a very good reason – if there is an important telephone call, a note on his desk is the best way to tell him.

What do you say if you're asked to collect a visitor from the waiting room? Something like this: 'Mr Smith? I'm Mr Adams' secretary. He asked me to show you to his office.' You lead the way, open the office door, say, 'Mr Smith for you, Mr Adams', stand aside to let the visitor pass and close the door behind him.

Incidentally, no good secretary need put up with bad manners from her boss since there are plenty of other employers who would give their eye-teeth for her services.

ON THE TELEPHONE

The correct and time-saving thing to do, whether you're ringing or being rung up, is to announce your identity at once: 'Blenkins and Company', 'Mr Adams' secretary', or whatever is appropriate. A secretary should never put a call straight through to her boss; she should get the caller's name and ask him to wait a moment while she sees if her boss is in – even though he may be sitting at the next desk.

If you are in a position to ask a secretary to get someone on the phone for you, you shouldn't keep them waiting when they come on the line. All too commonly done, this is extremely tactless.

PERSONAL TELEPHONE CALLS

Some firms don't allow them at all. Where they are allowed they should be kept to a minimum, since someone may be trying to get through on business and employees aren't paid to spend the morning quarrelling with their boy friends, or holding post mortems on last night's party.

MISTAKES

Everyone makes them occasionally, and the only thing to do is to admit them at once while there is still time to put them right. Even if, when you discover your mistake, it's too late to do anything about it, it's better to tell your immediate superior than leave him to find out for himself.

OFFICE POLITICS

Intrigues are part of the life of every firm. Mary thinks she should have had Jane's job and she is now busy stirring up all the hostility she can against Jane, trying to make the office so hot for her that she's forced to leave. However much you may sympathize with either Jane or Mary, the only wise course is to steer clear. Intrigues in an office may do enormous damage to the work output as well as creating a thoroughly unpleasant atmosphere, and sooner or later anyone who encourages them is out.

Men in the Office

As far as they're concerned you are simply a colleague. As soon as you enter the office you forfeit your feminine privileges. You do your own fetching and carrying, open your own doors and if you go out to lunch with them or for an after-work drink you will probably be expected to pay your share. If you ever come across a man who regards you as a woman first and a colleague second, beware before you plunge head-long and remember that if it comes to the point when you never want to see him again, you may have to resign your job.

Office Collections

Collections for leaving and wedding presents are a feature of most firms. Ideally contributions should only be solicited from people who know the girl in question. But in fact, you may very well be asked to stump up for someone you've met once and will never meet again within two weeks of your start in a new job, and unless you are extremely strong-minded, you will fork out. How much do other people give? In a large firm, most people work on the principle that if everyone gives a little, the result will be quite a handsome present and the average contribution, except in the case of a personal friend, is 5 or 10p; the boss may feel he ought to give a bit more. As you fork out your lunch money for the umpteenth time, console yourself – if you can! – with the thought that your turn will come.

Christmas and Birthday Presents

Beyond possibly finding 5p all round for a potted plant for the head of the department at Christmas time, no one in their right senses does anything about Christmas and birthday presents in the office. One present can so easily snowball into a tradition. Jane gives Mary a bottle of scent for her birthday, Mary feels she has to give Jane something on hers, and before the year's out, birthday presents all round have become office routine and a crippling expense for anyone on a small budget. More charitable to everybody in the long run is the curious custom that prevails in many firms for the girl whose birthday it is to buy a cake to hand round to her workmates.

Office Parties and Outings

The snare here is to remember in the midst of all the informal jolly eating and drinking that the boss, however much he's letting his hair down, is still the boss and that jokes at his or the firm's expense that seem innocent enough in the hilarity of the moment may look different when recollected by him the next morning.

Otherwise, manners at the firm's party should be the same as at any other party. You say goodbye and thank you to your host, unless he really doesn't know you're alive, or it's a very large party. Your men colleagues who, in the office, will happily watch while you struggle with an enormous pile of files, will spring into gallant action and expect to fetch and carry for you and light your cigarette.

Business Lunches

The woman who entertains people to lunch on behalf of her firm has long been an accepted part of the business scene. She arranges the seating at the table, orders and tastes the wine, and tells the waiter what her guests want to eat. Her guests expect her to pay, knowing that she will get her money back on expenses. But to save any possible embarrassment, many women have an account at the restaurant so that when the bill comes all they need do is sign it.

Giving Notice

The correct way is by letter. But if you're on friendly terms with your immediate superior it's polite to tell him first. Good policy, too; it gives him an opportunity to offer you a better job than the one for which you are leaving.

Rises

Gone are the days when you could wait modestly for your merit to be recognized by a rise. These days you usually have to demand it if you have no union to do this for you. If you think you are underpaid go to your boss and tell him so politely, giving your reasons. 'I have now worked for you for a year for X pounds a week. Everyone else I know doing the same job is getting five pounds a week more. I wonder if you could possibly give me a rise, Mr Blank?'

Christian Names

In some newspaper offices everyone from the big chief to the secretaries is known to everyone else by his or her christian name. In one well-known London shop women who have worked beside each other for years still address each other as Miss Blank.

The best policy here is to do whatever your colleagues on the same level in the firm's hierarchy do or, if you're the junior in a department where everyone else is much older, call them by their surnames unless or until they ask you not to.

CHAPTER 6

TITLES

How to Address Peers, Baronets and Knights

THE GROWING tendency towards informality and the feeling these days that a man should be honoured for his own achievements rather than those of his ancestors has made practically obsolete some of the traditional ways of addressing titled people. The styles listed under 'Formal Modes of Address' in this chapter are rarely used today except by employees and people on a much lower social level. The old-fashioned formal way to end a letter: 'I have the honour to be your obedient servant', etc, is practically never used now, 'Yours faithfully' being commonly used instead.

Envelopes of business letters are now usually addressed in the same way as envelopes for social letters.

The peers are, in order of precedence, Dukes, Marquesses, Earls, Viscounts and Barons.

DUKE
(For Royal Dukes see Chapter 13, 'High Life')

Social Forms of Address
  In speech. Introduce him as 'The Duke of — ', refer to him as 'The Duke', or 'The Duke of — ', address him as 'Duke'.
  In Writing. Begin 'Dear Duke of — ' or, if you know him fairly well, 'Dear Duke'. Address the envelope 'His Grace, The Duke of — ' or 'The Duke of — '.

Formal Modes of Address
  In speech. Refer to him as 'His Grace', address him as 'Your Grace'.

In writing. Begin 'My Lord Duke'.

DUCHESS

Social Forms of Address

In speech. Introduce her as 'The Duchess of — ', refer to her as 'The Duchess of — ' or 'The Duchess'. Address her as 'Duchess'.

In writing. Begin 'Dear Duchess of — ' or 'Dear Duchess'. Address the envelope 'Her Grace, The Duchess of — ' or 'The Duchess of — '.

Formal Modes of Address

In speech. Refer to her as 'Her Grace', address her as 'Your Grace'.

In writing. Begin 'Madam' or 'Your Grace'.

MARQUESS

Social Forms of Address

In speech. Introduce him, refer to him and address him as 'Lord (Leicestershire)'.

In writing. Begin 'Dear Marquess (of Leicestershire)' or 'Dear Lord (Leicestershire)'. Address the envelope 'The Marquess (of Leicestershire)'.

Formal Modes of Address

In speech. Refer to him as 'His Lordship', address him as 'My Lord' or 'Your Lordship'.

In writing. Begin 'My Lord'.

MARCHIONESS

Social Forms of Address

In speech. Introduce her, refer to her and address her as Lady (Leicestershire).

In writing. Begin 'Dear Marchioness (of Leicestershire) or 'Dear Lady (Leicestershire)'. Address the envelope 'The Marchioness (of Leicestershire)'.

Formal Modes of Address
> *In speech.* Address her as 'Madam' or 'Your Ladyship'. Refer to her as 'Her Ladyship'.
> *In writing.* Begin 'Madam'.

EARL

Social Forms of Address
> *In speech.* Introduce him, refer to him and address him as 'Lord (Wallingford)'.
> *In writing.* Begin 'Dear Earl (of Wallingford)' or 'Dear Lord (Wallingford)'. Address the envelope 'The Earl (of Wallingford)'.

Formal Modes of Address
> Same as for Marquess.

COUNTESS

Social Forms of Address
> *In speech.* Introduce her, refer to her and address her as 'Lady (Wallingford)'.
> *In writing.* Begin 'Dear Countess (of Wallingford)' or 'Dear Lady (Wallingford)'. Address the envelope 'The Countess (of Wallingford)'.

Formal modes of Address
> Same as for Marchioness.

VISCOUNT

Social Forms of Address
> *In speech.* Introduce him, refer to him and address him as 'Lord (Bellingham)'.
> *In writing.* Begin 'Dear Viscount (Bellingham)' or 'Dear Lord (Bellingham)'. Address the envelope 'The Viscount (Bellingham)'.

Formal Modes of Address
> Same as for Marquess.

VISCOUNTESS

Social Forms of Address

In speech. Introduce her, refer to her and address her as 'Lady (Bellingham)'.

In writing. Begin 'Dear Viscountess (Bellingham)' or 'Dear Lady (Bellingham)'. Address the envelope 'The Viscountess (Bellingham)'.

Formal Modes of Address

Same as for Marchioness.

BARON

Social Forms of Address

In speech. Introduce him, refer to him and address him as 'Lord (Inchworth)'.

In writing. Begin 'Dear Lord (Inchworth)'. Address the envelope 'The Lord (Inchworth)'.

Formal Modes of Address

Same as for Marquess.

BARONESS

Social Forms of Address

In speech. Introduce her, refer to her and address her as 'Lady (Inchworth)'.

In writing. Begin 'Dear Lady (Inchworth)'. Address the envelope 'The Lady (Inchworth)'.

Formal Modes of Address

Same as for Marchioness.

ELDEST SON OF DUKE, MARQUESS OR EARL

He bears by courtesy his father's second title. Thus the eldest son of a Duke may be a Marquess, the eldest son of a Marquess may be an Earl and the eldest son of an Earl may be a Viscount.

They and their wives are addressed in all respects as though their titles were 'actual' instead of 'courtesy' except that they should strictly speaking be addressed on envelopes without the prefix 'The'. Thus the son of a Duke who bears the courtesy title 'Marquess of X' should be addressed on an envelope simply as 'Marquess of X'.

ELDEST GRANDSON OF A DUKE OR A MARQUESS

He bears by courtesy his grandfather's third title. Thus the grandson of a Duke may be an Earl and the grandson of a Marquess a Viscount. They and their wives are addressed in all respects as though their titles were 'actual' except that strictly speaking they should be addressed without the prefix 'The' on envelopes.

YOUNGER SON OF DUKE OR MARQUESS

Social Forms of Address

In speech. Introduce him as 'Lord (John Smith)'. refer to him as 'Lord (John Smith)' or 'Lord (John)', address him as 'Lord (John)'.

In writing. Begin 'Dear Lord (John Smith)' or, if the acquaintance is more than slight, 'Dear Lord (John)'. Address the envelope 'Lord (John Smith)'.

Formal Modes of Address

Same as for Marquess.

WIFE OF YOUNGER SON OF DUKE OR MARQUESS

Social Forms of Address

In speech. Introduce her as 'Lady (John Smith)', refer to her as 'Lady (John Smith)' or 'Lady John'. Address her as 'Lady (John)'.

In writing. Begin 'Dear Lady (John Smith)' or, if the acquaintance is more than slight, 'Dear Lady (John)'. Address the envelope 'Lady (John Smith)'.

Formal Modes of Address
Same as for Marchioness.

UNMARRIED DAUGHTER OF DUKE, MARQUESS OR EARL

Social forms of Address
> *In speech.* Introduce her as 'Lady (Mary Jones)', refer to
> her as 'Lady (Mary Jones)' or 'Lady (Mary)'. Address
> her as 'Lady (Mary)'.
> *In writing:* Begin 'Dear Lady (Mary Jones)' or, if the
> acquaintance is more than slight, 'Dear Lady (Mary)'.
> Address the envelope 'Lady (Mary Jones)'.

Formal Modes of Address
Same as for Marchioness.

MARRIED DAUGHTER OF DUKE OR MARQUESS

If she marries a peer (i.e. the owner of an actual, not a courtesy, title) she is addressed according to the rank of her husband, also if she marries the eldest son of a Duke or a Marquess.

If she marries anyone else, she keeps her own title 'Lady (Mary)'. Thus if she married the eldest son of an Earl with the courtesy title of Viscount X, she would be known as Lady Mary X (though occasionally if she marries the eldest son of an Earl she may drop her own title and be addressed according to her husband's courtesy title). If she married the younger son of a Duke or a Marquess, 'Lord John Smith', she would be known as 'Lady Mary Smith'. If she married the younger son of an Earl or the son of a Viscount or Baron, 'Hon. Jeremy Brown', she would be known as Lady Mary Brown. If she married a Baronet or a Knight, 'Sir George South', she would be known as 'Lady Mary South'. If she married plain 'Mr Paul West', she would be known as 'Lady Mary West'. Except that she no longer uses her maiden name, she is addressed in the same way as an unmarried daughter of a Duke or Marquess.

MARRIED DAUGHTER OF AN EARL

If she marries an Earl's eldest son, she is addressed according to his rank, otherwise correct modes of address are the same as for married daughters of Dukes and Marquesses.

YOUNGER SON OF EARL, SON OF VISCOUNT OR BARON

Social Forms of Address

In speech. Introduce him, refer to him and address him as 'Mr (North)'.

In writing. Begin 'Dear Mr (North)'. Address the envelope 'Hon. (Alan North)'. ('The' before Hon. is often used but it is no longer considered strictly correct.)

Formal Modes of Address

In speech. Refer to him as 'Mr (North)', address him as 'Sir'.

In writing. Begin 'Sir'.

WIFE OF ABOVE

Social Forms of Address

In speech. Introduce her, refer to her and address her as Mrs (North).

In writing. Begin 'Dear Mrs (North)'. Address the envelope 'Hon. Mrs (Alan North)'.

Formal Modes of Address

In speech. Refer to her as 'Mrs (North)'. Address her as 'Madam'.

In writing. Begin 'Madam'.

UNMARRIED DAUGHTER OF VISCOUNT OR BARON

Social Forms of Address

In speech. Introduce her, refer to her and address her as 'Miss (North)'.

In writing. Begin 'Dear Miss (North)'. Address the envelope 'Hon. (Anne North)'.

Formal Modes of Address

Refer to her as 'Miss (North)'. Otherwise as for wives of younger sons of earls.

MARRIED DAUGHTER OF VISCOUNT OR BARON

In speech. According to the rank of her husband.

In writing. Begin according to the rank of her husband. Address the envelope according to her husband's rank if she marries a man of equal or higher rank than herself. If she marries a man of lower rank she keeps her own title. Thus, if she marries a baronet or a knight, she is addressed as 'Hon. Lady (Kinley)'; if she marries a commoner, as 'Hon. Mrs (Ffoulks)'.

WIDOW OF PEER OR BARONET

The general custom is to address her in the same way as when her husband was alive unless the present peer or baronet is married, in which event her own christian name is usually used in front of the title, on envelopes 'Henrietta, Duchess of X', 'Henrietta, Lady X', etc. But if she is the senior widow, she may prefer to be styled, 'The Dowager Duchess of X', 'The Dowager Lady X', etc. In speech and at the beginning of letters she is addressed as if her husband were still alive. If she marries again, she loses any title gained by her previous marriage.

DIVORCED WIFE OF PEER OR BARONET

She is styled 'Henrietta, Duchess of — ', etc, unless she remarries in which case she loses any title gained by her previous marriage.

BARONET

Social Forms of Address

In speech. Introduce him as 'Sir (Donald Kinley)', refer to him as 'Sir (Donald Kinley)' or 'Sir (Donald)', address him as 'Sir (Donald)'.

In writing. Begin 'Dear Sir (Donald Kinley)' or, if the acquaintance is more than slight, 'Dear Sir (Donald)'. Address the envelope 'Sir (Donald Kinley), Bt'.

Formal Modes of Address
  In speech. Refer to him as 'Sir (Donald Kinley)', address him as 'Sir'.
  In writing. Begin 'Sir'.

BARONET'S WIFE

Social Forms of Address
  In speech. 'Lady (Kinley)'.
  In writing. Begin 'Dear Lady (Kinley)'. Address the envelope 'Lady (Kinley)'.

Formal Modes of Address
  Same as for Marchioness.

KNIGHT

In the case of a knight of an order you must give him the appropriate letters after his name on an envelope, e.g. Sir (Alexander Williams) KBE, CMG. In the case of a knight bachelor, he may be addressed simply as 'Sir (Alexander Williams)'. Otherwise knights are addressed in the same way as baronets.

WIFE OF A KNIGHT

In the same way as for baronet's wife.

DAME

Social Forms of Address
  In speech. Introduce her as 'Dame (Margaret Green)'. Refer to her as 'Dame (Margaret Green)' or 'Dame (Margaret)'. Address her as 'Dame (Margaret)'.
  In writing. Begin 'Dear Dame (Margaret Green)' or 'Dear Dame (Margaret)'. The appropriate letters should always be added after her name on an envelope, e.g. 'Dame (Margaret Green) GBE'.

Formal Modes of Address

  In speech. Refer to her as 'Dame (Margaret Green)'.
  Address her as 'Madam'.
  In writing. Begin 'Dear Madam'.

The Church of England

ARCHBISHOP

  In speech. Introduce him as 'the Archbishop of — ', refer
  to him as 'the Archbishop of — ' or as 'the Archbishop'.
  Address him as 'Your Grace', both formally and socially
  or, if you're on very friendly terms, as 'Archbishop'.
  In writing. In a formal letter begin 'My Lord Archbishop'
  or 'Your Grace'. In an informal letter begin 'Dear Lord
  Archbishop' or, if you're on very friendly terms, 'Dear
  Archbishop'. Address the envelope, 'His Grace The Lord
  Archbishop of — '.

BISHOP

  In speech. Introduce him as 'the Bishop of — ', refer to
  him as 'His Lordship', address him as 'My Lord', both
  formally and socially. People on familiar terms with him
  may address him as 'Bishop'.
  In writing. In a formal letter begin 'My Lord' or 'My
  Lord Bishop'. In an informal letter begin 'Dear Lord
  Bishop', or more familiarly, 'Dear Bishop'. Address the
  envelope, 'The Right Rev. The Lord Bishop of — '
  except when writing to the Bishop of Meath who is
  addressed as 'The Most Rev.'.

Conventionally these modes of address are used for suffragan and overseas bishops as well as diocesan.

DEAN AND PROVOST

In speech. Introduce and refer to him as 'the Dean of—' or
'the Provost of—', address him as 'Mr Dean or 'Mr Provost'.

In writing. In a formal letter begin, 'Very Rev. Sir'. In a social letter begin 'Dear Mr Dean' or 'Dear Mr Provost'. Address the envelope 'The Very Rev. The Dean (or Provost) of — '.

ARCHDEACON

In speech. Introduce him and refer to him as 'the Archdeacon of — '. Address him as 'Mr Archdeacon.'

In writing. In a formal letter begin, 'Venerable Sir'. In a social letter begin 'Dear Mr Archdeacon'. Address the envelope 'The Venerable The Archdeacon of — '.

CANON AND PREBENDARY

In speech. Introduce him, refer to him and address him as 'Canon (Smith)' or 'Prebendary (Smith)'.

In writing. In a formal letter begin 'Reverend Sir'. In a social letter begin 'Dear Canon (Smith)' or 'Dear Prebendary (Smith)'. Address the envelope 'The Rev. Canon (or Prebendary) J. Smith'.

MINOR CANONS, RURAL DEANS AND OTHER CLERGY

In speech and letters. Introduce, refer to and address them as 'Mr Smith' (never as 'The Reverend' or 'the Reverend Smith'). Envelopes are addressed 'The Rev. (J. Smith)'.

WIVES OF CLERGY

Address them as plain 'Mrs', unless either they or their husbands have a secular title, in which case the normal rules apply.

The Navy

ADMIRAL OF THE FLEET

Address the envelope, 'Admiral of the Fleet (Sir John Smith)'. Otherwise address him according to his peerage or other rank.

ADMIRAL, VICE-ADMIRAL, REAR ADMIRAL

In speech. Introduce him as 'Admiral (Smith)' or, if he is a knight or baronet, as 'Admiral (Sir George Smith)'. Address him as 'Admiral (Smith)' or, if he is a knight or baronet, as 'Sir (George)'.

In writing. Begin 'Dear Admiral (Smith)', 'Dear Admiral' or, if he is a knight or baronet, 'Dear Sir (George)'. It is correct to give him his full title on the envelope: 'Admiral (Sir George Smith)', 'Vice-Admiral (Sir George Smith)', 'Rear' Admiral (A. E. Smith)', though socially the 'Vice' or 'Rear', is often omitted.

COMMODORE

In speech. Introduce and address him as 'Commodore (Smith)'.

In writing. Begin 'Dear Commodore (Smith)'. Address the envelope 'Commodore (J. N. Smith)'.

CAPTAIN

In speech. Introduce and address him as 'Captain (Smith)'.

In writing. Begin 'Dear Captain Smith'. Address the envelope 'Captain (J. N. Smith, DSO), RN'.

COMMANDER

In speech. Introduce and address him as 'Commander (Smith)'.

In writing. Begin 'Dear Commander (Smith)'. Address the envelope 'Commander (J. N. Smith) RN'.

LIEUTENANT-COMMANDER

In speech. Introduce and address him as 'Lieutenant-Commander (Smith)'.

In writing. Begin 'Dear Lieutenant-Commander (Smith)'. Address the envelope 'Lieut-Commander (J. N. Smith) RN'.

LIEUTENANT

In speech. Address him as 'Lieutenant (Smith)'.

In writing. Begin 'Dear Lieutenant (Smith)'. Address the envelope 'Lieutenant (J. N. Smith) R.N'.

SUB-LIEUTENANT

In speech. Address him as 'Mr (Smith)'.

In writing. Begin 'Dear Mr (Smith)'. Address the envelope 'Sub-Lieutenant (J. N. Smith) RN'.

MIDSHIPMAN

In speech. Address him as 'Mr (Smith)'.

In writing. Begin 'Dear Mr (Smith)'. Address the envelope either 'Midshipman (J. N. Smith) RN' or '(J. N. Smith) Esq. RN'.

CADET

In speech. Address him as 'Mr (Smith)'.

In writing. Begin 'Dear Mr (Smith)'. Address the envelope '(J. N. Smith) Esq. RN'.

The Army

FIELD-MARSHAL

Address the envelope, 'Field-Marshal (Lord —)'. Otherwise address him according to his peerage or other rank.

GENERAL, LIEUTENANT-GENERAL, MAJOR-GENERAL

In speech. Introduce him as 'General (Smith)' or, if he is a knight or baronet, 'General Sir (George Smith)'. Address him as 'General Smith' or 'Sir (George)'.

In writing. Begin 'Dear General (Smith)' or 'Dear Sir (George)'. It is correct to address the envelope 'General (Sir George Smith)'. 'Lieut-General (Sir George Smith)'. 'Major-General (J. N. Smith)'. Though socially Lieutenant and Major are often omitted.

E.G.M.—5

BRIGADIER

In speech. Address him as 'Brigadier (Smith)'.
In writing. Address the envelope 'Brigadier (J. N. Smith)'.

COLONEL

In speech. Address him as 'Colonel (Smith)'.
In writing. Address the envelope 'Colonel (A. E. Smith)'.

LIEUTENANT-COLONEL

In speech. Address him as 'Colonel (Smith)'.
In writing. Begin 'Dear Colonel (Smith)'. Address the envelope 'Lieut-Colonel (J. N. Smith)'. The regiment is added after the name preceded by any decorations.

MAJOR

In speech. Address him as 'Major (Smith)'.
In writing. Begin 'Dear Major (Smith)'. Address the envelope 'Major (J. N. Smith)' (name of regiment).

CAPTAIN

In speech. Address him as 'Captain (Smith)'.
In writing. Begin 'Dear Captain (Smith)'. Address the envelope 'Captain (J. N. Smith)' (name of regiment).

LIEUTENANT AND SECOND LIEUTENANT

In speech. Address him as 'Mr (Smith)'.
In writing. Address the envelope '(J. N. Smith) Esq.'. (name of regiment). His rank is used only on official and service envelopes.

The Royal Air Force

MARSHAL OF THE ROYAL AIR FORCE

Address the envelope 'Marshal of the Royal Air Force, (Lord —)'. Otherwise address him as for his peerage or other rank.

AIR CHIEF MARSHAL

In speech. Introduce him as 'Air Chief Marshal (Sir Alan Smith)'. If he is a knight or a baronet, address him as 'Sir (Alan)'.

In writing. Begin 'Dear (Sir Alan)'. Address the envelope 'Air Chief Marshal (Sir Alan Smith)'.

AIR MARSHAL

In speech. Introduce him as 'Air Marshal (Smith)' or, if a knight or baronet, 'Air Marshal (Sir Alan Smith)'. Address him as 'Air Marshal (Smith)' or 'Sir (Alan)'.

In writing. Begin 'Dear Air Marshal (Smith)' or 'Dear (Sir Alan)'. Address the envelope 'Air Marshal (A. E. Smith)' or 'Air Marshal (Sir Alan Smith)'.

AIR VICE-MARSHAL

In speech. Introduce him as 'Air Vice-Marshal (Smith)' or 'Air Vice-Marshal (Sir Alan Smith)'. Address him as 'Air Vice-Marshal (Smith)' or 'Sir (Alan)'.

In writing. Begin 'Dear Air Vice-Marshal (Smith)' or 'Dear (Sir Alan)'. Address the envelope 'Air Vice-Marshal (A. E. Smith)' or 'Air Vice-Marshal (Sir Alan Smith)'.

AIR COMMODORE

In speech. Introduce him and address him as 'Air Commodore (Smith)'.

In writing. Begin 'Dear Air Commodore (Smith)'. Address the envelope 'Air Commodore (A. D. Smith)'.

GROUP CAPTAIN

In speech and writing. Address him as 'Group Captain (Smith)'. Address the envelope 'Group Captain (A. E. Smith)'.

WING COMMANDER

In speech and writing. Address him as 'Wing Commander (Smith)'. Address the envelope 'Wing Commander (A. E. Smith)'.

SQUADRON LEADER

In speech and writing. Address him as 'Squadron Leader (Smith)'. Address the envelope 'Squadron Leader (A. E. Smith)'.

FLIGHT LIEUTENANT

In speech and writing. Address him as 'Flight Lieutenant (Smith)'. Address the envelope 'Flight Lieutenant (A. E. Smith)'.

Below this rank Air Force titles are not used socially.

Other Dignitaries

AMBASSADOR

In speech. Formally he is addressed as 'Sir' or 'Your Excellency' and referred to as 'His Excellency'. Socially he is addressed as for his private rank, as 'Sir (John)' or 'Mr (Smith)'.

In writing. The formal way to begin is 'Sir' or according to his rank; the social way is 'Dear Sir (John)' or 'Dear Mr (Smith)'. Address the envelope 'His Excellency, The British Ambassador', 'His Excellency, Sir (John Smith, KCMG)' or 'His Excellency (John Smith, CMG)'.

AMBASSADOR'S WIFE

In speech. Formally she is sometimes addressed as 'Your Excellency' and referred to as 'Her Excellency', but she is more often addressed as for her private rank, as 'Lady (Smith)' or 'Mrs (John Smith)'.

In writing. Begin 'Madam', 'Dear Lady (Smith)' or 'Dear Mrs (Smith)'. Address the envelope 'Her Excellency Lady (Smith)', 'Her Excellency Mrs (John Smith)' or simply 'Lady (Smith)' or 'Mrs (John Smith)'.

But when they are in this country an ambassador and his wife are addressed as for their private rank only.

LORD MAYOR

Letters are addressed 'The Rt. Hon. The Lord Mayor of — ' in the case of the Lord Mayors of London, York, Belfast, Sydney (N.S. Wales), Melbourne (Victoria), Adelaide (S. Australia), Perth (W. Australia), Brisbane (Queensland) and Hobart (Tasmania). To other Lord Mayors the envelope is addressed 'The Right Worshipful The Lord Mayor of — '. Address him formally both in speech and at the beginning of a letter as 'My Lord'. Address him socially as for his private rank.

LORD MAYOR'S WIFE OR LADY MAYORESS

Address the envelope 'The Lady Mayoress'. Otherwise address her as for her private rank.

MAYOR

In speech. On the bench a mayor is addressed as 'Your Worship', otherwise as 'Mr Mayor' or, socially, according to his or her private rank.

In writing. Begin a formal letter 'Dear Mr Mayor', a social letter 'Dear Mr (Smith)' or 'Dear Mrs (Smith)'. If the mayor of a city, address the envelope 'The Right Worshipful The Mayor of — '; if the mayor of a borough, 'The Worshipful the Mayor of — '.

MAYOR'S WIFE

On formal official occasions she is sometimes addressed as 'Mayoress'. Otherwise address her as for her private rank.

JUSTICES OF THE PEACE

When on the bench address them as 'Your Worship'. On a letter addressed to them in their official capacity, add the letters JP after their name. Otherwise address them as for their private rank.

CHAPTER 7

TALKING

THIS IS not a book on grammar, but you can't discuss saying the right thing at the right time without mentioning it. Today more than ever before kind hearts are worth more than coronets and a generous sentiment is more valuable than the language that clothes it – but certain snobberies about the use of language still linger on, especially among the middle-class middle-aged. You may win friends, but you are unlikely to influence people if, for instance, you are constantly using double negatives. The double negative as in, 'I can't come here no more', instead of the correct, 'I can't come here any more', brands the user as illiterate. Other common bad mistakes are: the use of 'me' instead of 'I' and vice versa, as in 'You and me think alike', and 'between you and I' instead of the correct, 'You and I think alike', and 'between you and me'.

But curiously enough there are some grammatical errors to which society has given its blessing. They are not merely accepted, but anyone who used instead the grammatically correct form would be considered pedantic. The answer to 'Who's that?' is usually, 'It's me', instead of the grammatically correct, 'It's I'. Similarly it is incorrect, but usual to say, 'That's her', or 'That's him' and, 'Who did you give it to?' Split infinitives – e.g. 'to quickly run' – have also come to stay and are so generally used as no longer to be particularly noticeable.

Accents

The pendulum of fashion has swung with a vengeance. Nowadays an exaggerated public school accent can be a positive disadvantage to a young man or woman looking for a job, at least in the field of human relations. Local accents have invaded the BBC, that one-time bastion of the Queen's English and are to be found on most company boards. And so fashionable did the Beatles make the Liverpudlian accent that many young people deliberately cultivated it. Socially, however, among the middle-class middle-aged, local accents apart from Scottish (non-Glaswegian) and Irish are still frowned on – and most particularly the cockney accent. Also still derided among this small section of society is the 'genteel' or 'refained' accent, by which I mean the pronunciation of 'nice as 'naice', 'home' as 'haome', 'now' as 'naow', 'oh' as 'aoh', probably because it is a bad imitation of the public school one.

The words you use

A few years ago certain words revealed a person's whole social background. Since Professor Ross and Miss Nancy Mitford turned the spotlight of public attention on 'U' and 'non-U', they have ceased to be so indicative. 'Loo', once a 'U' euphemism for lavatory, is now as generally used by speakers from all social backgrounds as are 'bye-bye' and 'kids', once strictly 'non-U' expressions. There are still, however, a few words and expressions that are peculiar to the different social strata and, while one set of terms is no better than the other, it is easier to use the language of the people you are mixing with at the time – as many a school child learns. The boy who uses the term 'lavatory' in the local primary may be ridiculed quite as much as the boy who uses the word 'toilet' at a prep school.

On the left are the words and expressions used by the upper-income groups, on the right those used by the lower.

'What did you say?'   'Pardon'
'Sitting room'   'Lounge' (though U.I.G.s
                         talk about the hotel lounge)

'Sofa'	'Couch' (though U.I.G.s talk about the psychoanalyst's couch)
'Lunch'	'Dinner' (for the midday meal)
A 'drive' in his car	A 'ride' in his car
'Riding'	'Horse-riding'
Lavatory (in a restaurant, they ask for the 'ladies cloakroom')	Toilet
'The tall man over there', also 'the tall old man'	'The tall gentleman over there'
'Bathing suit'	'Bathing costume'
'Suit'	'Costume'
'Scent'	'Perfume'
'Vegetables'	'Greens'
'False teeth'	'Dentures'
'Jam'	'Preserve'
'Please may I have . . .'	'Can I trouble you for . . .'
'Begin'	'Commence'
'Table napkin'	'Serviette'
'Make a remark'	'Pass a remark'
He died	He passed away

Foreign Words

'Parliament having *d'oré la pillule* his Royal Highness is to swallow it . . .' wrote Sarah, Lady Lyttelton in a letter in 1809; and, 'We shall see the good Aumales tonight, who are staying with the Van de Weyers at New Lodge, which is *un vrai bijou* . . .' wrote Queen Victoria in 1860. In the last century it was fashionable to lard conversation and letters with as many French words and phrases as possible.

Now that going abroad is no longer confined to the upper classes, it is considered affected to use a foreign word where an English one will do and, in the case of words that have been absorbed into the English language, to give them their original pronunciation when there is an anglicized version. *Valet, Paris* and *cul de sac* for instance are pronounced as spelt. *Chauffeur* is pronounced *shofur*, *bouquet* as *bukay*, *champagne* as *shampain*. The words have become part of our language and it would be quite wrong to treat them as though they were still French.

Where on the other hand there is no anglicized version – you can't, for instance, anglicize Champs Elysées – there is nothing for it but to get the pronunciation right or avoid the word altogether.

Introductions

There are two basic rules for introductions. (1) The man is always introduced to the woman, except when he is a much older or more important person. You would introduce a young girl to a bishop and not the other way round. And you would introduce the new typist to the director of the firm. (2) When both are of the same sex, the junior is always introduced to the senior person; a young girl is introduced to a middle-aged woman, a young man to an older man.

Except with royalty (see Chapter 13) no one uses the old-fashioned 'May I present . . .' More usual are: 'Mrs Bloggs, I don't think you've met Mr Smart,' 'Mrs Bloggs, do you know Mr Smart?' or 'Mrs Bloggs, this is Mr Smart.' In these forms the person whose name is said last is the person who is being introduced.

But introductions are becoming less and less formal. At parties today, your hostess is most likely to say simply, 'Mary Bloggs, Jane Smith,' which has the advantage, when two people are of the same sex and age, of not making it clear whom you are introducing to whom.

MEMBERS OF THE FAMILY

They are exceptions to the rule. Members of the family should be introduced to non-members of the family, unless there is a great discrepancy in age or status. A man taking his wife to his firm's annual party should introduce her to his colleagues, 'Mr

Smith, I don't think you've met my wife; Mary, this is Mr Smith.' It is considered very bad form for a husband or wife to introduce each other as Mr or Mrs to people on the same or a higher social level.

If on the other hand a young girl brings her boy friend down to spend the weekend with her parents, she would say, 'Daddy and Mummy, this is John', introducing the boy friend to them since they are so much older.

WHEN YOU FORGET A NAME

What should you do when, as you are about to introduce someone, their name goes clean out of your mind? Resourceful people have been known to say heartily, 'This is my very best friend. And here is Mary Smith.' And cowards to murmur, something unintelligible: 'Mary Smith', and vanish hastily to another part of the room leaving Mary Smith to find out his name for herself. Another trick is partial honesty: 'It's idiotic of me but your surname has just slipped out of my head. I know it so well . . .' This is usually less offensive than| forgetting his christian name, which is more personal. With luck, he'll supply the missing christian as well as surname at the same time.

Alternatively, you can hum and haw several times before introducing the person whose name you've forgotten. Usually they will say their own name out of sheer self-preservation!

AT PARTIES

The best hostesses are those who don't simply say, 'Mary Smith, John Jones', and leave them wondering how on earth to start a conversation, but give some sort of cue. It doesn't really matter how slight. 'Mary's mad about tennis, too', or, 'John's a lepidopterist', may not lead the way to sparkling witticisms but it does at least give Mary and John a particle of knowledge to build on.

And if Mary doesn't know what lepidopterist means she can always start the conversation by asking him.

IN THE STREET AND IN RESTAURANTS

Suppose when you're with a friend in a restaurant or in the street you see someone you know? If you greet the person and pass on, it's unnecessary to do any introducing. But if you stop for a long chat, it's obviously bad manners to leave your friend out of the picture and you must introduce him or her.

Greetings

The formal thing to say when you meet someone for the first time is, 'How do you do'. This is just a more polite way of saying 'Hallo' and the correct reply is also 'How do you do', not 'Very well, thank you' or 'My feet are killing me'. 'How are you?' is usually just as meaningless, but it does seem to require some kind of answer. Most people settle for 'Very well, thank you' or 'fine, thank you'.

What you are never supposed to say, if you are middle-class and middle-aged, is 'Pleased to meet you' – but 'I'm so pleased to meet you' is strangely enough considered okay.

Shaking Hands

When to shake hands? Always, if someone offers to shake hands with you. Unlike other nationalities, we tend not to shake hands at parties – a boon to women who need three hands anyway, one for their handbag, one for their drink and one for their cigarette. Handshakes among the young are becoming uncommon on all occasions except as a mark of very special friendship, but there are no rules. People do whatever seems the friendliest or most courteous thing at the time.

Small Talk

The woman who believes in remaining silent unless she has something worthwhile to say is a social wet blanket. Small talk is essentially light-hearted and superficial and it is much more important to keep the ball in the air than to produce a memorable remark. Never answer a question with a simple 'No' or 'Yes' or 'I don't agree', always contribute something of your own that can serve as a cue to the next speaker.

The topics to bring up at a social gathering are those likely to entertain and interest the particular company. That is why subjects acceptable at a women's coffee party are boring at a drinks party to which people go in the hope of escaping from the daily round. Sure-fire topics are any in the news – Wimbledon if it's Wimbledon week, the current strike and that case in the law courts; good small talkers are avid newspaper readers. Books, films and plays can be useful subjects too.

Of course, there are some talkers so entertaining that they can afford to hold forth on a subject about which the rest of the party know nothing. But, if no one else is allowed to get a word in, they have got to be really entertaining or they will be considered bores. Most of us would selfishly rather sparkle ourselves than watch other people sparkling – which is why a shy person can get by very well if she sticks to asking other people's opinions and listening appreciatively to the answers.

Subjects to Avoid

Politics, religion and sex, the Victorian taboo subjects, are mentioned today at most social gatherings but they do need tactful handling. Because the point of the Victorian taboo remains a valid one: it is bad manners to spark off a violent row or to embarrass people. So before you launch an attack at a dinner party on a particular political party or religious denomination, do make sure your fellow guests share your sympathies. Similarly though sex is no longer the sacred cow it was, over-frank remarks on this subject can still be embarrassing in mixed company.

Another Victorian taboo was that 'nice people don't discuss other people'. This is now completely outdated. One of the easiest ways to start a conversation is to talk about a mutual friend. Though it is obviously tactful to keep your comments complimentary, at least until you know what sort of relationship exists between the person you are talking about and the person you are talking to. It's all too easy to mention 'the girl in the terrible dress over there' only to find she's his wife.

Gossip is one of the mainstays of small talk and one usually finds those who deride it most indulge in it just as much as everyone else. Everyone can't talk intelligently on films and books, but they can express interest in the fact that John Smith is getting married to that pretty model.

Gossip need not necessarily be malicious, though the sad truth is that it is much easier to be amusing about people's faults than their virtues. But ethics apart, anyone who goes in for malicious gossip must be prepared for it to get back to its subject as it almost invariably does.

Money

While it is no longer bad form to mention money, this is a subject almost guaranteed to cast gloom over any social gathering; for most people – who haven't got enough of it – the thought of money is worrying and depressing. And for those few who do have plenty of money, to have the limelight focused on their affluence can be embarrassing.

It is still in bad taste to boast about your earnings and tactless to ask anyone but an intimate friend a direct question: 'How much did that dress cost?'; 'What did you pay for your house?' or, 'How much do you earn?'

Shop

This is another Victorian taboo that is no longer valid. Whether you should talk shop or not today depends not on etiquette but how the person you are talking to feels about it. Many people enjoy talking about their jobs and are more interesting on this subject than on any other. Inviting them to talk shop may give them an opportunity to shine which they would not otherwise get.

But people who don't particularly enjoy their jobs or who work very hard at them may prefer to get right away in their leisure hours. Doctors and psychiatrists for instance rarely want to talk about medicine or psychiatry at a party. Again people who do some highly specialized work may not want to discuss it with those who know nothing about it.

One time when it *is* bad manners to talk shop is in a small gathering of people most but not all of whom belong to the same profession, since those who don't will be left out of the conversation.

Class and Colour

For idealistic reasons, these are the new taboo subjects among the under forties. 'Class', suggesting that some people are better than others, sticks in their gorge with the result that even the term 'middle class', which for many years now has been used to indicate both what used to be called the 'middle and the upper classes' is itself avoided as far as possible. The young substitute such euphemisms as 'upper income groups' and 'lower economic strata'. Words like 'coloured' are also generally avoided, because of their racialist undertones. The tactful way to refer to people whose names you don't know is by their place of origin, such as 'African' or 'West Indian'. 'Asian' is a useful word when you don't know whether someone is Indian, Pakistani or Bangladeshi.

Tactless Questions

People are less secretive about their ages than they were. Victorian mothers often disguised their ages even from their own daughters. But it is still not tactful to ask anyone over the age of thirty, 'How old are you?' And if you do ask you are five out of ten times not going to get a truthful answer. Pretending to be twenty-nine may not make one a day less than thirty-five, but many women still persist in the myth that by ignoring time they can cheat it. Even when they are plainly elderly some women still go on lying about their age. And not only women. Men often knock off a year or two for the sake of their careers or simply an almost feminine vanity.

'When are you two going to get married?' This again is not a tactful question. But it's frequently asked all the same. The chances are either that he hasn't asked her or that they have been arguing hotly on the subject for some time. A useful reply is a light-hearted, 'We're just good friends', which is so hackneyed that it can mean anything.

Apologies

Apologies are embarrassing to both parties and in any case can't undo the damage. The best policy is to say you're sorry once as though you really meant it and leave it at that. The person apologized to is supposed to say, 'It doesn't matter', sounding as sincere as she can even though her precious Sèvres vase lies shattered at her feet.

Interrupting

This is a very common fault, but it is bad manners. Good manners require you to let the other person finish regardless of the fact that by that time the funny story you were about to tell may no longer be appropriate.

Contradicting

There are comparatively tactful ways of pointing out that someone's under a mistaken impression, but a flat contradiction is not among them. A sentence beginning, 'That's wrong', or, 'That's not true', may come to exactly the same thing as a sentence that begins, 'Don't you think that . . .', but the former is a great deal ruder and more likely to lead to raised tempers.

Swearing

Now that four-letter words are used uncensored in print and on television, can the individual use them with impunity? The answer is that it depends on the company. Constant use takes the shockingness out of swear words, their original meaning is forgotten and they become just a noise that expresses our feelings when we are annoyed.

But since one of the criteria of good manners is to avoid offending other people's susceptibilities, before you give voice to your favourite expletive, it is advisable to consider whether it will be as meaningless to the people you are with as it is to you. And incidentally the men who are themselves heavy swearers are often just as horrified as Aunt Mary to hear women follow suit, women's lib or not.

Slang

Use of the current slang has become a kind of status symbol proving that one is truly contemporary and up to date. The trouble is that so many people are always a little behind. There is something ridiculous about the middle-aged desperately scrambling to seem young, to use the latest word and always just missing it, still using 'fabulous' when 'super' has come in and 'super' when the young are saying 'great' or 'good' or 'nice'.

Americanisms

Many of the young now use I *guess* instead of I *suppose*; *sure* instead of *yes certainly*; the pronunciation *skedule* for *schedule;* and *formidable* instead of *fórmidable*. Aided by American films and the mass media who seem to think American is modern – as well as the American books used to teach our own children to read in state schools – Americanisms are flooding into the English language. Against this, the educated middle-classes fight an often strongly felt but losing battle. The American language is successfully invading ours and winning ever more general acceptance.

What to Say if You are Asked to . . .

. . . PRESENT PRIZES

It is unnecessary to say more than a very few introductory words along these lines: 'I am sure we all feel delighted at the great success of . . .', or, 'It gives me great pleasure to hand the prizes to the successful competitors'; if the competition is a children's obstacle race, you could add, 'who certainly fully deserve them!'

If the winner is well known to everyone present you could say something about him or her or, if you like, something about the competition or something about the qualities needed for success.

. . . INTRODUCE A SPEAKER

Begin with some welcoming phrase such as: 'We are very pleased to have Lady Smith with us today and flattered that, in spite of her numerous engagements, she has found time to fit us in.' Give reasons why Lady Smith is so well qualified to speak on the subject of her forthcoming address. Finish by saying, 'Ladies and gentlemen, Lady Smith.'

. . . PROPOSE A VOTE OF THANKS

This can be very brief, simply: 'I have much pleasure in proposing a vote of thanks to Lady Smith for her most interesting talk.' If you like you can add some comment on any aspect of the talk you found particularly interesting.

Addressing a Meeting

The formal way is to begin: 'Ladies and gentlemen' unless distinguished people with titles are present in which case these are mentioned first. If the Queen were present you would begin, 'Your Majesty, Ladies and Gentlemen'; if a member of the royal family, 'Your Royal Highness, Ladies and Gentlemen'; if a Duke, Duchess or Archbishop, 'Your Grace, Ladies and Gentlemen'; if a peer, 'My Lord, Ladies and Gentlemen'; if a Lord Mayor, 'My Lord Mayor, Ladies and Gentlemen'.

Where only women are present the form is simply, 'Ladies'. Where just one man is present the usual form is, 'Mr Smith, Ladies . . .'

Toasts

Toasts after lunch or dinner are proposed when coffee has been served, by the chairman if there is one, the senior man present or anyone else specially qualified. If the dinner is in honour of a special guest something complimentary should be said about him or her, and the particular reason for celebrating should be mentioned. A brief re-cap of the guest's achievements or services may be appropriate, also humorous recollections and allusions likely to appeal to the listeners. The toast is proposed at the end of the speech. The proposer holds up his glass and says simply, 'Mr Blank'.

Everyone present except the person or people toasted then stands up to drink his or their health.

What do you do if there is nothing left in your glass ? Simply tilt it and pretend; it's all symbolic anyway.

A toast normally calls for a reply in a similar vein, though the opportunity may be taken to add or emphasize some personal views on a serious subject.

At a formal dinner, the person replying to the toast would not propose another toast. But on a less formal occasion people please themselves; at a wedding reception, for instance, the bridegroom replies to the toast to the bride and groom and usually ends by proposing a toast to the bridesmaids.

Here are some useful stock phrases: 'It is my pleasant duty to propose the toast to — '; 'It is my privilege to propose the toast to — '; 'I have been honoured by being asked to propose the toast to — '; 'I know you will all want to join with me in drinking to the success of — '.

Tip for anyone faced with making a speech for the first time: keep it short. The following reply to a Toast to the Guests coming at the end of a succession of long speeches went down extremely well:

'Though I may not look as young as I am, this is the first time I have been asked to make a speech. I know there is one quality in maiden speakers that always wins the applause of the audience, and that is brevity. So I will simply say on behalf of the guests, thank you, thank you very much.'

A TOAST TO THE LADIES

Unless one of them has been asked beforehand it is not generally considered necessary for them to reply. Though, of course, one of the ladies can retaliate by proposing a toast to the gentlemen!

CHRISTMAS TOASTS

Some families who have an annual get-together at Christmas like to round off the meal with toasts usually proposed by the senior member of the family; a toast to the Queen, a toast to Absent Friends, and a toast to the hostess. These toasts are not usually preceded by speeches.

COMING-OF-AGE PARTY

The old friend of the family who proposes the toast says something complimentary about the boy or girl, refers to the importance of the age of eighteen and finishes by wishing him or her every happiness and success.

The hero or heroine of the hour need only reply very briefly saying: 'Thank you for all the nice things you have said about me and thank you all for your good wishes'. Though they can if they like, of course, make a longer speech.

CHAPTER 8

WRITING

'THERE IS no greater opportunity to show good taste – or bad – than in the type of notepaper you use' states a 1920s etiquette book. And even today, among middle-class people, certain taboos about personal writing paper persist. Any colour other than white, cream, grey or blue they consider bad taste, and the same goes for rough or scalloped edges, coloured borders and pretty pictures; paper with ruled lines they think only suitable for children. They consider plainness synonymous with good taste. The envelope should fit the folded paper neatly and match it in colour and texture. Needless to say, even the most snobbish person would rather have a letter from a friend – even if it is written on the wrong sort of paper and stuffed into the wrong kind of envelope – than not.

Headed Writing Paper

Printed headings are usual for business and are increasingly used on personal writing paper; they can look very attractive in a well-designed print. However, among the middle-class it is still 'smarter' to have your address and telephone number engraved.

The usual colours for engraved headings are blue on blue paper, red on grey paper, black or blue on white or cream paper. It should be set either in the centre of the top of the page or in the right-hand top corner, the lettering absolutely plain, all capitals being more usual than capitals and small letters e.g.:

STICKLEBACK MANSIONS
  BELTON SQUARE
    LONDON SW3 4LF
   TEL. OI – 352 9225

28 ABERCROMBY GARDENS
HOVE
SUSSEX
    BN3 8UA

When the address is in the right-hand corner, the telephone number is sometimes put across the opposite left-hand corner – one solution in these postcode days to addresses that seem to go on for ever.

For brief notes some people use a small sheet of writing paper with the address and telephone number engraved or printed along the width, e.g.:

   19 PUTLEY STREET, LONDON, SW3 4LF OI–352 2345

Layout for a Personal Letter

The first essential is that it should be as pleasant as possible to look at – a short letter should be centred in the middle of the page, never bunched up at the top with an ugly waste of space beneath the signature.

When the address is hand-written or typed the date is usually, but not always, put directly underneath. When the address is engraved, people fit the date in where they can.

In formal letters, people give the year as well as the day and month, 27th June, 1973 or 27/6/73; in letters to close friends, people often simply scrawl Saturday or Wednesday. The 'Yours sincerely' etc should begin underneath the last sentence of the letter, in the centre of the page.

Layout for a Business Letter

The name and address of the person you are writing to should be put on the left-hand side of the page either below your own address or below your signature. This is the conventional way to set out any letter on business, whether typed or hand-written:

19 Putley Street,
London SW3 4LF
January 5th, 1973

The Manager,
Plum and Bodsworth Ltd,
Appleton Square,
London, WIN 9UZ

Dear Sir,

Or:

Yours faithfully,

The Manager,
Plum and Bodsworth Ltd,
Appleton Square,
London, WIN 9UZ

Typed Private Letters

Many professional people find it more convenient to type their private letters than to write them by hand. But there is a rather cold, impersonal feeling about a typewritten letter – especially if the writer has a secretary and there is a chance he may simply have dictated it. One way to get over this impersonal feeling is to hand-write the 'Dear Mary' or 'Dear Mr Smith' and also the 'Love from' or 'Yours sincerely' and add a few words by hand at the bottom of the letter.

But letters of condolence being of a very personal nature should be hand-written throughout.

Addressing the Envelope

Name and address should be roughly in the centre of the envelope. When they are typed they may either be indented or put one underneath the other:

> Mrs A. B. Smith,
> The Grange,
> Little Newington,
> Reading,
> RG8 0DT

When they are hand-written it is usual to indent:

> Mrs. A. B. Smith,
> The Grange,
> Little Newington,
> Reading,
> RG8 0DT

It is not considered correct to write the address or any part of the address in quotation marks, e.g. 'The Grange'. Whenever possible the postcode should be placed on a line by itself at the end of the address. A clear space, the width of at least one character, should be left between the two halves of the postcode, the letters should not be joined and the code should include no punctuation. The commas at the end of each line of an address are in any case today increasingly left out.

ESQUIRE

The days when 'Esq.' was used only after the name of a member of the upper classes and everyone else was addressed as 'Mr' are no longer with us. The safe general rule for anyone who doesn't want to risk giving offence is to address all untitled men as 'Esq.' regardless of status or family tree.

'John Smith, Esq.', is the usual form when you know his christian name, if you don't, you give him his initials, 'J. S. Smith, Esq.'.

What should you do when you don't know his initials? Since some people, for some unknown reason consider '— Smith, Esq.' bad manners, the only solution is to guess.

MARRIED WOMEN

The old-fashioned rule that the senior married woman of the family was addressed as 'Mrs Smith', the others as 'Mrs (husband's christian name or initials) Smith' is now rarely observed, since it entails knowing all about the family. 'Mrs (husband's christian name or initials) Smith' is the usual style of address for all married women today.

WIDOWS

They are addressed in exactly the same way as when their husbands were alive. (For widows of peers and baronets see Chapter 6.)

DIVORCED WOMEN WHO HAVE NOT RE-MARRIED

Address them by their own christian name or initials and their ex-husband's surname, 'Mrs Mary Smith'.

PROFESSIONAL MARRIED WOMEN

Letters sent to them in their professional capacity are usually addressed 'Mrs (her own christian name and husband's surname)'

ADDRESSING HUSBAND AND WIFE TOGETHER

Write: 'Mr and Mrs (husband's christian name or initials) Smith'.

UNMARRIED WOMEN

Formerly, the rule was that the senior unmarried woman in the family was known simply as 'Miss Smith', the others as 'Miss Mary (or initials) Smith'. This is rarely observed today, the usual style of address for all unmarried women being 'Miss Mary (or initials) Smith', although creeping in from America and the women's lib movement is a new style designed to diminish the difference between the married and the unmarried state: Ms in place of Miss or Mrs. But before using this new style it is worth remembering that some females are almost as strongly anti-women's lib as others are pro.

Two sisters together are still addressed as 'The Misses Smith'.

CHILDREN

Girls are addressed as 'Miss Mary (or initials) Smith', boys simply as 'John (or initials) Smith'. Occasionally as 'Master John Smith'.

CARE OF

It is considered good manners when you write to a friend staying in someone else's house to include the name of her hostess on the envelope:

> Miss Mary Smith,
> c/o Mrs John Brown,
> The Grange.

MESSRS AND LTD

It is incorrect to use them both on the same envelope. A limited company should be addressed as 'Jones and Brown Ltd.' 'Messrs.' should be used only when addressing a partnership, 'Messrs. Jones and Brown'. But when the name of a partnership is preceded by 'the' or a title, 'Messrs.' is not used, e.g. 'The British Blanket Company', 'Sir John Smith & Co.' If you don't know whether a firm is a partnership or a limited company, it is perfectly correct to write the name of the firm, 'Jones and Brown', and leave it at that.

Beginnings

Most people today begin plain 'Dear' both to lifelong friends and to strangers. 'Dear Sir or Madam' is the form when you don't know the sex of the person you are writing to, 'Dear Sirs' when you are writing to a corporate group of people, such as a shop, rather than an individual.

Endings

Those most generally in use today are 'Love from' to intimate friends and relations, 'Yours' to people you address by their christian name but don't know well enough to send your love to, 'Yours sincerely' to anyone you address by their surname, whether social or business acquaintances, 'Yours faithfully' when the letter begins 'Dear Sir' etc. A cordial note is often lent to 'Yours sincerely' by the addition of 'Best wishes' or 'Kind regards'.

At the end of a typed business letter it is usual to type your name and, if you are writing on behalf of a firm, your position, under your signature, 'Mary Smith, Features Editor'. If your letter is hand-written and the person you are writing to doesn't know whether you are Miss or Mrs, it is usual to add it in brackets beside your signature, 'Mary Smith (Mrs)'.

Letters after People's Names

These fall into three categories: Crown Honours — that is any orders or decorations, whether for civil or active service, conferred by the Queen; membership of learned societies, etc; and letters indicating academic distinctions, professional or official status. Letters after a name should be written in the order given in the reference books.

CROWN HONOURS

These should be added on an envelope unless you know that the person you are writing to prefers not to use them. But if someone has a whole string of letters after his name, the letters standing for the most distinguished honour or honours only need be used. Though some people with minor honours only, such as an MBE, prefer not to use them, unless you know that it is courteous to add them. But if a man has a minor crown honour and also a relatively much greater distinction in another field, you might leave out the crown honour. When writing to a man with an MBE who is also a Fellow of the Royal Society, for instance, you might give him his FRS and leave out the MBE.

MEMBERSHIP OF LEARNED SOCIETIES

Letters standing for membership of learned societies, etc, are added usually only if they imply special distinction. (For letters standing for professional qualifications see paragraph below.) You would add FRS (Fellow of the Royal Society), FBA (Fellow of the British Acadamy), FSA (Fellow of the Society of Antiquaries of London), RA (Royal Academician) ARA (Associate of the Royal Academy) for instance, but not FRHistS (Fellow of the Royal Historical Society) or FRGS (Fellow of the Royal Geographical Society).

LETTERS INDICATING PROFESSIONAL OR OFFICIAL STATUS AND ACADEMIC DISTINCTIONS

QC (Queen's Counsel) and MP should always be added. PC (Privy Councillor) is not used when addressing anyone below the rank of Marquess, The Right Hon. being used as a prefix instead. Other letters indicating professional or official status are not generally used in private correspondence, but they should be used when writing to their owners in an official or professional capacity. Letters denoting Masters' or Bachelors' degrees, MA, BA, BSc, etc, are rarely used except when writing to someone in the teaching profession.

Content of Letters

Gone is the idea that a letter should be written in a careful prose style that bears little relation to speech. True, most people are more careful of their grammar when they are writing than when they are talking, but otherwise the fashion is for letters to be as colloquial as possible. 'Can't', 'shan't' and 'won't' are now written as well as spoken and it is no longer considered impolite to write '&' for 'and'.

All this, however, has not altered the fact that certain types of letters are still tricky for those faced with writing them for the first time.

Thank-You Letters

It's time-saving as well as good manners to write them as promptly as possible. Two brief paragraphs are perfectly acceptable if you write immediately. But if you put it off for several weeks, you should write a longer letter.

BREAD-AND-BUTTER

After spending a night in someone else's house, however sincerely you may have said thank you when you left, you should still write a thank-you letter. One sentence of thanks followed by a description of your life and loves since is not generally considered enough except to intimate friends. The form is to say why you enjoyed yourself and to mention any aspect of your stay which gave you particular pleasure.

Here is a letter from a girl who had been to stay with her boy friend's parents:

Dear Mrs Smith,

   I did so enjoy my weekend with you. It was a real treat for me to get out of London into the country – such a lovely part of the country, too – and a wonderful rest from my usual weekend chores. The Point to Point was great fun – it is the first time I have been to one.

  The roads were surprisingly clear on the way back. Tom and I got to London in under an hour.

  Again, thank you so very much.

Yours sincerely,
Mary Brown.

THANK YOU FOR A PRESENT

Like bread-and-butter letters the best thank-you-for-a-present letters contain more than one sentence of thanks. The form is to say why the present is just what you wanted, 'though we have received seven clocks and three electric toasters, until your present arrived we had not got a single saucepan', or to give some sort of picture of it in use, 'the vase looks lovely against the red walls of our sitting room and cheers us up whenever we look at it'.

Letters of Condolence

It is impossible to lay down any hard and fast formula for a letter of condolence. Obviously your own personal feelings and the character of the person you are writing to must be your guide. But most of us are so unaccustomed to expressing our deep feelings on paper that the following tips may help.

The purpose of a letter of condolence is to console the living and the way to do that is not to harp on the tragic aspects of death but if possible to find the silver lining in the cloud. 'I am sure that is the way he would have liked to have died' is far more consoling than 'What a terrible way to end!' If you can refer to any happy memories of the dead man or woman, the full and happy life they led, or the good that they did, that will help, too.

The most difficult letter of condolence to write is to someone you don't know very well. Here is an example:

I felt I had to write and tell you how sorry I was to read of your mother's death. We both have very happy memories of our visits to 10 Godfrey Street. What a wonderful old lady she was, so up-to-date and interested in everything. I only hope I shall get as much out of life as she did, if ever I reach her age.

I know there is no real consolation, but please believe me that you have all our sympathy.

Letters of Congratulation

Congratulations on an appointment, an honour or passing an examination run very much to a pattern. You begin by saying how delighted you are to hear the news, go on to say how well he or she has deserved whatever it is and why.

Business Letters

Except in a few long-established firms which cling to the old forms, business letters no longer have a language all their own. Commercialese like, *Awaiting the favour of your reply*, *I oblige*, *Thanking you in anticipation* and *Re yours of the 20th ult* has gone out of fashion. Most business letters today begin, *Thank you for your letter of September 20th*, or, *In answer to your letter of September 20th*.

People who use long-winded phrases like *In order to obviate time wastage on either part*, instead of simply *So as not to waste time*, impress nobody but themselves. The way to write a good business letter is to state your case as simply and clearly as possible, e.g.:

LETTER TO A BANK

Dear Sir,
    Please will you pay the enclosed cheques into my account.

Yours faithfully,
Mary Smith (Mrs)

LETTER OF COMPLAINT TO A SHOP

Dear Sirs,
    On Monday June 20th, I bought a navy blue and white skirt price £11 at your shop. The label said drip-dry. I followed the washing instructions carefully, but in spite of this the navy blue has run into the white and the skirt is now completely unwearable.

    I would be grateful if you would give me a credit note for the cost of the skirt or return my money.

Yours faithfully,

Invitation Cards

The whole business of invitation cards is fraught with tricky little points of middle-class etiquette that, trivial or old-fashioned though they may seem, are still very widely observed by this stratum of society. (Readers who have no wish to seem middle class may prefer to skip this section.)

Which kind of card out of the large and confusing variety in the shops, in every sort of lettering on every sort of paper, should you choose? According to the middle-class code the following are incorrect: deckled edges, cocktail glasses, wedding bells, horseshoes and other jolly or sentimental decorations, however suited to the occasion. As with writing paper, the rule is: the plainer, the better. Lettering should always be black, never silver or coloured, on plain, good-quality paper.

The middle-class etiquette of invitation cards has changed very little during the last few years. But one concession has been made to modern budgets. Though it's grander to have your cards engraved, it is no longer a social solecism to have them printed. Brides' mothers faced with the enormous expense of even the simplest wedding have gone on strike. Invitations to all but the most fashionable society weddings today are printed, as are invitations to many cocktail parties. But cards are still engraved for very formal occasions such as coming-out dances and elaborate dinner parties.

Lettering on an engraved card should be copperplate, letterpress script on a printed card.

LITTLE POINTS

Here are some of the details that distinguish the most 'correct' cards. The day and the month should be given, but never the year, Saturday June 3rd, never Saturday June 3rd, 1973. There is a school of thought which claims that the RSVP should always be on the right hand side, but some of the cards sent out by the 'best' people have the RSVP on the left.

ENVELOPES

The strictly correct thing to do, when sending an invitation to a married couple, is to write the wife's name only on the envelope. But young people today when inviting friends of their own age usually disregard that rule and address the envelope to both.

Today the envelope is usually sealed since there is no longer any financial advantage in leaving it unsealed.

GUESTS' NAMES ON CARDS

A married couple are addressed as *Mr and Mrs John Smith*. If you want to invite the children as well, you add, *and family*. A single man is addressed as *Mr John Smith*. If you are inviting two sisters, Mary and Belinda Smith, *Miss Belinda Smith* is written under *Miss Mary Smith*.

If you were inviting a Duke and Duchess you would write *The Duke and Duchess of (Hampstead)*. All other peers and peeresses are addressed as *Lord and Lady (Hampstead)*. Baronets and knights and their wives are addressed as *Sir John and Lady (Smith)*. When a woman with a title in her own right is married to a commoner, you address them as *Mr John and Lady (Mary Smith)*.

The prefix Hon. and letters after names are never used on invitation cards.

In the case of a married couple where the husband has a clerical or service rank, the form is *The Bishop of (Barchester) and Mrs (A. E. Smith)*, *Admiral and Mrs (A. E. Smith)*. A doctor and his wife are addressed as *Dr and Mrs (A. E. Smith)*, a vicar or rector and his wife as *The Rev. and Mrs (A. E. Smith)*.

When a man has both a service rank and a title, usually only the title is used on the card. Admiral Sir John and Lady Smith would be addressed simply as *Sir John and Lady Smith*.

WEDDING INVITATION

This should be a folded white sheet of paper with the information engraved or printed on the outside and the guests' names hand-written in the top left-hand corner. The bridegroom's full name is given but only Christian names of the bride. The rest of the information should be given as briefly as possible as in the example below.

Sir Anthony and Lady Douglas

Mr and Mrs David Hedges
request the pleasure of your company
at the marriage of their daughter
Mary Rose
to
Mr John Maxwell Harding
at St Margaret's, Westminster
on Saturday, June 3rd
at 2 o'clock
and afterwards at
the Hyde Park Hotel

The Old Grange,
  Grampton,
    Reading,
      RG3 0DT   RSVP

It is becoming more and more usual for divorced parents to join forces for a daughter's wedding, in which case the invitation begins:

Mr James Brown
and
Mrs Paul Armstrong
request the pleasure of your company

When the bride's mother is on her own the invitation begins:

Mrs Peter Danvers
requests the pleasure of your company
at the marriage of her daughter

If the host and hostess are the bride's uncle and aunt, the invitation begins:

> Lieut-Colonel and Mrs Simon Brownlow
> request the pleasure of your company
> at the marriage of their niece

When for some reason the guests are to be invited to a reception only – perhaps the church is too small to hold everyone or the wedding is in a register office – the invitation begins:

> Mr and Mrs Jeremy Johns
> request the pleasure of your company
> at a reception
> after the marriage of their daughter

The best person to advise you on layout if you want any variation on the traditional wording is your printer.

COCKTAIL PARTY INVITATIONS

The correct cocktail party invitation when it is filled in reads like this:

Mr & Mrs John Smith
> Mrs Peter Potts
> at Home
> Thursday, May 11th
>> Drinks
>> 6 o'clock

23 Elm Square,
  SW3 4LF   RSVP

On the grandest cards Mrs Peter Potts, at Home, RSVP and the address are engraved and the other details hand-written in. But equally acceptable and less expensive are cards that have the at Home and RSVP only engraved or printed. Before they are filled in, these cards look like this:

....
at Home

....
RSVP

Formally, when a married couple give a party – except a lunch, dinner or wedding reception – only the name of the hostess should appear on the invitation card. But for informal parties, where everyone is on Christian-name terms, many people today dispense with this tradition and send out cards that read like this:

John & Mary Smith
           Peter and Jane Green
          at Home
       Friday, May 12th
                Drinks
23 Elm Square,   6 o'clock
  SW3 4LF   RSVP

Similarly, young unmarried men and girls sending invitations usually call themselves simply, 'Mary Smith' or 'John Smith', without a Mr or Miss, addressing older guests only as 'Mr and Mrs John Smith', people of their own age as plain 'John Smith' or 'Mary Smith'.

DINNER PARTY INVITATIONS

An At Home card may be used with the word Dinner in place of Cocktails. Or an engraved or printed card may be sent which, when filled in, reads like this:

> Mr and Mrs John Smith
> request the pleasure of
> Mr and Mrs Gerald Brown's
> company at dinner on Tuesday
> January 3rd at 7 o'clock

Milton Hall,
   Hampworth,
      Buckinghamshire.   RSVP

On a specially engraved card the names of the guests, the day, the date and the time only are written in by hand. On the ready-printed cards that can be bought in the shops the names of host and hostess and the address are also written in.

COMING-OF-AGE PARTY INVITATION

The form for such an invitation is:

> Mr and Mrs John Smith
> request the pleasure of the company of
> ....
> to celebrate the Coming of Age
> of their daughter
> Mary Rose
> at the Park Lane Hotel, London W1,
> on Saturday, March 25th
> Dancing 9 o'clock

14 Elm Square,
   SW3 4LF   RSVP

BOTTLE PARTIES

Rarely given now except by students and the very young, invitations are usually by telephone or word of mouth.

DANCE INVITATIONS

For an informal dance an ordinary At Home card can be used, filled in in exactly the same way as for a cocktail party except that 'Dancing' and the time the dancing is to start is put where the word 'cocktails' or 'drinks' usually goes. For a formal dance all the information is engraved and the card is larger.

When the dance is not being given at the address guests are to RSVP to, the card reads like this:

Miss Carolyn Poultney Smith
Lady Brown
at Home
Wednesday, May 20th
Hyde Park Hotel, Knightsbridge

RSVP
26 Elmbond Square   Dancing 10 o'clock
   SW3 4LF

When the dance is shared the card reads like this:

Lady Brown
Mrs John Smith
at Home
Wednesday, May 30th
Hyde Park Hotel, Knightsbridge

RSVP
  26 Elmbond Square,   Dancing 10 o'clock
    SW3 4LF

For a coming-out dance, invitations may be as above or they may include the girls' names, e.g.:

Lady Brown and Mrs John Smith
at Home
for
Mary Anne and Amanda
Friday, April 20th
at the Hyde Park Hotel, Knightsbridge

RSVP
  The Grange,   Dancing 10.15
    Little Upton,
      Sussex.

ANSWERING INVITATIONS

A formal invitation in the third person is answered in the third person and should repeat the occasion and the date like this:

> Mr and Mrs John Smith have much pleasure in accepting Mrs Alan Brown's kind invitation to a cocktail party on Tuesday, May 2nd.

Or:

> Miss Mary Smith has much pleasure in accepting Mr and Mrs Alan Brown's kind invitation to the wedding of their daughter on Saturday, July 20th.

This is written in the middle of the paper. If your writing paper has not got an engraved or printed heading, the modern fashion is not to write your address or the date of your reply.

If your writing paper is a large size and your acceptance looks ridiculously lost, you can fill it up by repeating the address where the party is to be held, or the name of the church.

What should you do if you receive an invitation card on which you are addressed simply as, 'Mary Smith'? Then you write back in the same style, 'Mary Smith has much pleasure in accepting Alan Jones's kind invitation', etc.

REFUSING A FORMAL INVITATION

It is considered polite to give a reason why you can't go, keeping it brief and in the third person.

> Miss Mary Smith very much regrets that she is unable to accept Mr and Mrs Alan Brown's kind invitation to the wedding of their daughter on Saturday, July 20th, owing to a previous engagement.

Other stock excuses are, 'owing to illness', and 'because she will be away on holiday'.

Invitations should always be answered as soon as possible so that your hostess can estimate her numbers.

Other Cards

CHRISTMAS CARDS

The modern fashion is to leave out the 'Mr' and 'Mrs' and write 'from John and Mary Smith' to all but the slightest acquaintances, even though you may not address them in speech by their Christian names. Of course, people sending cards to close friends sign only their Christian names. Some people have their addresses printed inside the card – a boon to friends whose address filing system may not be too good.

The envelope of a Christmas card may be left unsealed.

When the card is being sent to a married couple, both names appear on the envelope.

CHOOSING YOUR CARD

The sordid truth is that many people look on Christmas cards as an opportunity to show off their own taste and to judge that of their friends. If you belong to this category the cards to beware of are those covered in tinsel and gold and those with original 'poems' inside. A simple message such as 'Best wishes for Christmas and the New Year' is far safer than any original effort. Absolutely safe good-taste-wise are reproductions of famous paintings, preferably religious, since Christmas is after all a Christian festival.

But more and more people are choosing the most attractively designed card whether it has anything to do with Christmas or not. Another growing tendency is to send cards with a photograph of your house or your children.

What should you do if you receive a card from a friend you have accidentally left off your list? There isn't much you can do; no one writes a thank-you letter for a card.

But you may be among the growing number of people who have decided that Christmas cards are too expensive. If so, it is tactful to tell friends whose feelings might otherwise be hurt: 'We have decided not to send any cards this year'.

POSTCARDS

There is nothing against beginning, 'Dear Jim' and ending, 'Love, Mary', but most people don't. They simply say what they have got to say and sign their name or initials. 'Looks lovely, doesn't it. But wait till you hear. John & Mary.'

The great thing to remember when writing postcards is that, unlike letters, everyone feels entitled to read them.

CORRESPONDENCE CARDS

These are extremely useful for short business notes as well as brief messages to friends. Postcard size, they have the name and address of the sender printed along the top like this: 'From Mrs M. E. Brown, The Grange, Little Upton, Herts'. They can be sent as postcards, in which case the address is written on one side and the message on the other, simply signed 'Mary Brown' or 'M.B.' without any 'Dear Sirs' or 'Yours faithfully'. Or they can be treated like ordinary writing paper and sent in sealed envelopes. The telephone number is often included either on the same line as the address or beneath it.

What to serve depends on your purse. Guests expect to be given something they don't eat every night at home. That means they expect something more expensive or more elaborate or more unusual; but not necessarily all three together.

Good idea though it may seem, however, to use a dinner party as an excuse to experiment with an exotic new recipe rather than spending four hours and half the housekeeping trying it out on the family, experienced hostesses resist the temptation. Even the best recipes have unexpected hazards. Witness the case of a young wife who thought to impress her husband's boss with a recipe for chicken with almond sauce only to find just before he was due to arrive that the recipe included the words, 'pound the nuts'. She was still pounding the nuts an hour later.

Tinned and Packet Foods

Frozen vegetables appear at even the 'best' dinner tables, including Buckingham Palace, but fresh if you have time to prepare them are much nicer. Tinned and packet food tend to be heavily disguised to make them 'partified'. Most hostesses rely on them but rarely admit it. Guests who guess the secret – that the basis of this fabulous soup is just dear old Heinz chicken and mushroom after all – keep their discovery to themselves. Many hostesses, however, do feel it's worth making their own mayonnaise as well as real coffee, since these do taste quite different from the shop and instant varieties.

The Menu

Variety is the spice of a good meal as well as of life and the golden rule when planning the menu is to avoid repetition; potted shrimps, for instance, should not be followed by salmon, a pastry main dish by a pastry sweet, meat with a cream sauce by strawberries and cream. Colours as well as flavour and texture should be varied. Meat in a white sauce looks more

appetizing accompanied by peas and carrots than by white
vegetables such as leeks and boiled potatoes.

The Drink

The conventional hostess allows up to half an hour or so for
guests to relax with a drink before dinner. A glass of dry or
medium sherry – wine experts say it should be slightly chilled
but most hostesses serve it as it comes out of the bottle – or a
choice of sherry, whisky and gin and something, if she can
afford it.

At a four-course banquet guests are usually served two wines
one with the fish, another with the meat, possibly sherry with
the soup and, if they're lucky, liqueur or brandy after dinner.
But at the informal dinner party at home the most most hostesses feel called on to provide is one kind of wine served with
the main course. A safe estimate is one bottle between three or,
if guests are heavy drinkers, one bottle between two. But you
can get by with less if you serve a very special wine or give your
guests plenty to drink before dinner. Whether to provide anything to drink after dinner depends again on your purse. It's
not generally expected, but it may be a welcome surprise.

Here are some sample menus for beginners, including sug-
gestions for wine to serve with the main course.

Dinner Menus

Melon with ham or with ginger
Chicken Paprikash (chicken with a paprika and
cream sauce), rice, French beans
Apricot tart
Wine: Saint-Emilion

Avocado pear with oil and vinegar sauce
Roast pork, ratatouille (vegetable stew with aubergines,
onions and tomatoes), roast potatoes
Fruit salad made with white wine
Wine: Alsace Riesling, Traminer or Meursault

Shrimp cocktail
Osso Buco (pieces of veal stewed with
white wine etc.), rice
Home-made ice cream with raspberry sauce accompanied
by meringues or macaroons
Wine: Puligny-Montrachet or Alsace Riesling

Hot Weather Menu

Iced cucumber soup
Salmon, peas, new potatoes
Strawberries (serve them stalks removed, piled in a bowl,
sprinkled with sugar) and cream
Wine: Serve any dry white wine with the fish. Or serve
champagne with both the main course and the sweet.

Laying the Table

The most formal way to clothe a dinner table is with a white
cloth. For informal parties most people use mats on a polished
surface. (For how to lay the cutlery see page 131.)

One of the old etiquette rules rarely observed today even at
banquets is that butter should not be served with rolls at dinner
and that the rolls should be laid on a table napkin instead of on
a plate. Butter and bread plates appear on most dinner tables
today.

Wine glasses are normally laid above the knives; when there
are to be several wines, the largest glass is usually put on the
outside, but there is no hard and fast rule. (Water and water
glasses are not laid when wine is served). If port is to be drunk
with the dessert, port glasses are put with the other glasses on
the table.

Traditionally, liqueurs and brandy are served at the same
time as the coffee after the meal in the sitting room, so the
glasses should not strictly speaking be laid on the table.

Table napkins are simply folded and laid square to the edge

of the table. Linen napkins are nicest but coloured paper ones have taken their place in most households.

At a big dinner party it saves a lot of passing if there is more than one salt and pepper pot.

When fruit is eaten after the sweet, fruit knives and forks are brought in on the dessert plates if it is a formal dinner. At the informal dinner, guests are usually expected to eat the fruit with their fingers.

In any case not many housewives these days possess fruit knives and forks. The movement is towards fewer and fewer implements; bread plates or any suitable small plates stand in for the old-fashioned curved salad plates, teaspoons do for coffee, egg and grapefruit as well. The great silver chests of Victorian times with special implements for every conceivable purpose are a thing of the past. Few people have the space to store them all or the time to clean them.

FISH KNIVES AND FORKS

These, for most people, are something they see only in restaurants. Their use has never been universal and, a few years ago, was the subject of class snobbery. They have never appeared at Buckingham Palace, where the royal plate dates from before the time fish knives and forks were introduced; and the Edwardian and Victorian upper classes used to regard them as vulgar. Today few inheritors of a beautiful set of silver fish knives and forks would be put off using them by such old-fashioned snobbery; but no one need feel obliged to buy the things if they haven't already got them.

TABLE DECORATIONS

The best kind are small enough to allow guests a clear view of each other over the top. It's disconcerting to try and talk to someone you can see only dimly the other side of the wood. The classic decoration is a posy in a little round vase.

DECANTING AND DISHING UP

This is a question of aesthetics rather than etiquette. Food that comes in an ordinary glass bottle, jar, tin or cardboard container looks more attractive turned out on to a dish. But there is no need to decant anything that comes in an attractive container – preserved ginger, for instance, looks perfectly nice in its own jar.

Aluminium saucepans are out of place on the dinner table, but there are plenty of coloured casseroles in the shops that look just as attractive in the dining room as they are serviceable in the kitchen; and when the hostess is doing all the work they save a long pause in the meal while she dishes up.

Certain foods are always served in the dishes in which they have been cooked: soufflés, steak and kidney pudding (a napkin is wrapped round the basin) and pies.

Serving without help

The women are served before the men – the most important woman, if there is one, first, the most important man, if there is one, before the other men. Apart from this the criterion is speed and simplicity rather than etiquette. The main course is normally served in the dining room, the quickest way being for the hostess to serve out the meat while the etceteras, vegetable dishes and any gravies and sauces, are put on the table for guests to help themselves. The first course and the sweet are often brought in ready served on to the plates, except when this would spoil the look of a special dish, like a soufflé or a tart.

It is the host's job to do any carving; if it's a bird, he gives white meat to the women, dark meat to the men, if there isn't enough white to go round. But at a large party it's not a good idea to serve something that needs carving as, by the time the host has finished, the guests' food is either cold or they are ready for second helpings.

The host also pours the wine and any drinks before or after dinner.

Even at the most informal dinner people usually prefer to turn their backs on the dinner table and adjourn to another room or at least to comfortable chairs for coffee. But how to get them to move? There they sit, large grown-up people round your table, talking their heads off, apparently quite comfortable where they are. How on earth are you ever to transport them into your sitting-room simply by the power of words? The usual formula is: 'Shall we go into the other room for coffee?' And if they don't hear the first time, you take your courage in both hands and repeat it loudly. Conventionally, coffee pot, sugar basin and cream jug are brought in with small after-dinner coffee cups on a tray, and guests are asked whether they would like it 'black or white.'

Serving with Help

For a sit-down meal with a large number of guests some kind of help is essential; but the etiquette of serving varies according to what kind of help it is. The formal dinner party routine with trained staff is to serve straight round the table, irrespective of sex. If there are two waiters with duplicate dishes, one can begin with the woman on the host's right, then the host and so on, the other with the man on the hostess's right, then the hostess and so on. Alternatively, one can begin with the woman on the host's right and serve straight down that side of the table, while the other waiter serves straight down the other side of the table, beginning with the woman on the host's left – in which case host and hostess are served last.

Food is handed and plates are taken away on the left of each guest, but wine is poured on their right.

When there are not duplicate dishes the waiter may still serve straight round the table, beginning with the woman on the host's right, host and so on – or the women may be served first as at the dinner party without staff.

But the formal dinner party routine with trained staff is something few hostesses have to cope with unless they are married to an ambassador or work in the catering trade. In private life the only assistance most hostesses can get is distinctly untrained – the daily woman, a teenage daughter or the *au pair*. In this case what the hostess usually does is to serve the meat herself while her assistant hands round the vegetables; gravies and sauces are put on the table for guests to help themselves.

At a large dinner party, if you are serving a joint or a bird and you have help, it saves time if you have the meat carved in the kitchen and brought on a dish already cut up.

If there is a man servant, he pours the wine, otherwise this is still the host's job.

Guests

Six or eight is the usual number at an informal private dinner party. Invitation cards are only sent for very large or very formal dinners, the usual procedure being to invite people – preferably equal numbers of men and women – by telephone, at least a week in advance if your guests are likely to be busy. In a house, the hostess shows the women guests up to her bedroom to leave their coats and tidy up, the host shows the men to the downstairs cloakroom. In a small flat the men's coats go in the hallway, on a peg, a chair, or over the banisters, and the bathroom is usually too obvious for anyone to need to be shown where it is.

The way to get the party off to a good start is to lose no time getting your guests sitting down with a drink in their hands. Dinner is usually served around eight o'clock.

SEATING GUESTS

Traditionally at a rectangular table the host sits one end, the hostess the other, but many hosts and hostesses prefer to sit opposite each other at the middle of the table. The most important woman guest sits on the host's right, the next most important on his left, the most important male guest on the hostess's right, the next most important on her left; the least important guests sit furthest away from host and hostess.

Where no one is more important than anyone else, it still saves time and confusion if the hostess tells people where to sit, arranging men and women alternately and dividing husbands from wives. At large parties the easiest way is to put a card with a name on it at each place, christian names if you're on christian name terms with your guests, otherwise 'Mr Brown' and 'Mrs Smith'.

Going to a Dinner Party

If the hostess says, 'Come at eight o'clock', the perfect guest arrives dead on time. If she comes before, she may find her hostess in the bath; if she comes after, she may find the dinner is spoilt. Even the sweetest-natured hostess who has watched a soufflé shrink from frothy perfection to a piece of dull yellow leather while she waited for a latecomer is liable to swear that she'll never ask that person to dinner again.

But if your hostess says, 'Come at half past seven for eight o'clock', that means dinner won't be served till eight, the first half hour will be taken up with drinks, so guests can be a little late.

GOING IN TO DINNER

At grand official dinners people still go in two by two, usually host and most important lady first, hostess and most important man last. But at private dinner parties the women go into the dining room first, followed by the men.

OFFERING TO HELP

All guests at the dinner party without staff help stacking plates at table, and passing things round. Whether they should do anything further depends on their hostess. There are hostesses who expect their guests to help wash up, but there are many more who really prefer to see their guests enjoying themselves rather than labouring over the kitchen sink and putting everything away in the wrong place. The best rule is: when in doubt offer, but don't press.

Hostesses coping with the problem of guests who insist on helping in spite of all protests can always take refuge in the white lie that the daily will do it in the morning.

Again there are some hostesses who appreciate help with the fetching and carrying and final touches. But they're few and far between. All too often the guest who insists on coming into the kitchen and lending a hand is just another problem. Instead of being able to concentrate on stopping the meat from burning, the sauce from curdling and taking the sprouts off at just the right moment, the hostess has to make bright conversation or think up things for the other woman to do.

REMARKS ON THE FOOD

Old-fashioned etiquette says never. This still applies at the banquet level. But when a hostess has done the cooking herself and taken a lot of trouble over a special dish, it's discouraging to have it passed over in polite silence as though it were simply meat and two veg.

WITHDRAWING

This old-world custom is still observed in a few households. If your hostess rises and murmurs, 'Shall we?' while the men sit tight, that is your cue to follow her out of the room and leave the men to their port. The women follow the hostess up to her bedroom to tidy up and discuss babies and clothes. The men join them for coffee and liqueurs in the sitting room anything up to half an hour later.

Today it is most usual for men and women guests to remain together throughout the evening. But some hostesses compromise with the old etiquette, asking after dinner: 'Would anyone like to come upstairs?' This gives women a chance to go to the upstairs lavatory and men a chance to disappear into the downstairs 'gents' before going into the sitting room for coffee.

WHEN TO GO

The formal time to leave after an eight o'clock dinner is 10.30 to 11. But there are some hosts – mostly those who don't have to get up early the next morning – who feel the party's been a failure if guests don't stay on at least until midnight.

SAYING THANK YOU

You should thank your hostess when you leave and most people telephone her within the next day or two to repeat their thanks and say how much they enjoyed themselves. If you want to be extra polite you can write to your hostess instead of telephoning.

The Informal Buffet Dinner Party

This kind of party is growing in popularity; it suits the new casual approach to entertaining and enables a hostess to have more guests than she could otherwise accommodate. Guests sit where they like, next to whom they like, and eat off their laps instead of sitting round the dining table. Food tends to be simpler and less expensive – two courses instead of three is the usual number: a hot dish (chili con carne or goulash or curry, for instance) followed by a cold pudding. Food, plates and cutlery are put on the table for guests to help themselves and people also often help themselves to the wine – usually plentiful but cheap. Old-fashioned courtesy requires that 'a gentleman' should always see the woman's plate and glass are filled first but this is a rule often ignored by the younger generation.

Guests are invited either by telephone or At Home card. The buffet dinner usually begins at eight o'clock, but there is a growing custom to serve a buffet dinner at the end of a cocktail party. In which case it is considerate to warn guests beforehand so that they don't either leave a joint to burn in the oven or eat a large tea first.

Formal Buffet Meal

The food, including usually cold meats, salad, and various aspics and mousses, is laid out on a snowy white cloth on a long sideboard and served by the waiters or waitresses behind it. Guests indicate what they want.

How to give a Cocktail Party

At the best cocktail parties the room is full but not too full for both guests and drink to circulate. A small knot of people in a large empty room is not conducive to the party spirit, but neither is a crush similar to rush hour in the tube. People tend to get frozen in the same little groups all evening because it's too hard work to move.

Traditionally a cocktail party is a stand-up affair and it's a mistake to have too many chairs. When half the guests are sitting and the other half standing, a party splits into two.

THE TIME

Either before lunch from 12 to 1 or before dinner from 6.30 to 8. Since few people can get away from work on a weekday morning, the before-lunch cocktail party is usually confined to Saturdays and Sundays – after church on Sunday morning is fashionable in the country. The advantage of the before lunch party is that guests arrive and leave more promptly. At a lively evening cocktail party they tend to stay on until either the drink runs out or they get hungry, which is usually nearer nine than eight.

INVITATIONS

For a small party, invitations are made by telephone. For a large party, it's quicker to send At Home cards, see page 124. How much notice to give depends on how crowded the diaries of the people you invite are likely to be. Three or four weeks is average for a large party, a fortnight for a small one. If you give a spur-of-the-moment party the chances are that the people you want most, your dearest friends, the wittiest men and the prettiest girls, will be otherwise engaged and you will find yourself spending a lot of time and money on comparative strangers or people nobody else wants to entertain.

Giving good notice also allows you to balance your numbers. Ideally the sexes should be nearly equal, erring on the side of a few extra men. But too many men can be as fatal as too many women. Either the competition becomes unsociably fierce or they give up the struggle and retire into small masculine huddles to talk about cars.

THE DRINK

The conventional drinks are: sherry (dry or medium); whisky; gin with French vermouth, tonic, lime juice or orange squash; Dubonnet. Some people serve 'cup' as well – or instead – of the more expensive drinks. Alternatively, today you can serve wine only – a fashion which is growing among young people in London; it is usual to offer a choice of red or white wine (both dry). A lavish variant on the conventional cocktail party is to serve champagne only.

Estimating how much drink people will get through is extremely difficult – one person will hang on to the same drink all evening and another will quaff it like water. A good way to avoid either running out or getting left with a lot of unwanted bottles is to buy on a sale or return basis. Unopened bottles go back and your money is refunded.

At a small cocktail party it is the host's job to fill up the glasses while the hostess moves round with the eats. At a large party this is not feasible. The best, but expensive, solution is to have waiters walking round with trays. The next, is to inveigle a friend into acting as unpaid barman. Otherwise the only answer is to have the drink and glasses all on one table and leave guests to help themselves, which usually they show no reluctance in doing. The host, if he's to talk to his guests at all, can't hope to do more than see that everyone gets something to drink when they arrive and to fill up the odd glass here and there.

THE FOOD

Since the driver no longer feels entitled to drink very much, the dutiful hostess of today feels she ought to offer something more substantial than the odd handful of salted nuts, crisps or stuffed olives to justify his presence in her sitting-room. Hard work though they are, an ingenious variety of titbits on sticks and canapés (relying heavily on substitutes for caviare and smoked salmon) are coming back into favour, ousting the once more popular, delicious but messy dips. Children above the age of six prove surprisingly obliging on these occasions and come in useful for handing round the food.

THE ASH PROBLEM

A feature of every other party is the guest who remarks with a fatuous grin that it's good for the carpet. The practised hostess provides against this by dotting ashtrays all round the room. When they're all at one end, even the best-intentioned guest may find himself dropping ash on the floor.

Some cigarettes are sometimes on the house, decanted out of their packets into cigarette boxes or wine glasses, although this custom is not so widespread now that many people have given up smoking.

LOOKING AFTER GUESTS

It happens to most hostesses. The food's ready, the drink's ready, she's ready. It's long past time for the party to begin and still no one has turned up. Perhaps no one will turn up at all and all her preparations have been for nothing. But invariably they do turn up, usually in a rush and then there are a hundred things to do at once.

The first thing to do is to let guests know where they can put their coats – customarily there is one room with a mirror for the women, another place for the men. The next thing is to see that the new arrivals get something to drink and someone to talk to; general introductions are possible only when there are only a few people in the room.

The perfect host and hostess are constantly on the go, circulating among their guests, saying a few words to each, seeing that as nearly as possible everyone gets introduced to everyone else and nobody gets stuck with one person except from choice.

But this can be carried too far. At some parties no sooner have you been introduced to a man and got past the preliminaries of asking him what his name is, you didn't quite catch it, when you're spirited off to be introduced to someone else and have to begin all over again.

Going to a Cocktail Party

A peculiarity of the cocktail party is that guests are not expected to arrive on the dot. The best time to get there is about quarter of an hour late. There is nothing against arriving later except that you will probably find yourself facing a room full of strangers several drinks ahead of you while you're still cold sober.

The procedure is to dump your coat first, then go in and greet your hosts who will find you a drink and someone to talk to.

CIRCULATING

The most unrewarding type of guest from the host's point of view is the one who sits in a corner gossiping with the same person all evening. Guests are supposed to circulate, one of the delights of a cocktail party being that you may find yourself talking to an artist one minute and someone in the soap business the next. Male guests are supposed to talk to female guests and vice versa. Where the two sexes divide into separate groups the party spirit is killed stone dead. Married couples are supposed to split up; when they arrive their hostess should, if she has time, make sure that each has someone different to talk to.

How to get away from the man who seems bent on talking to you and you only all evening? The accepted and perfectly polite way is to say firmly: 'Excuse me, I must go and talk to Tom.' The coward's escape is to wait until he offers to get your glass filled up, then nip off and be deep in conversation with Tom when he returns. But the buttonholer's motive may be not your superior charm but the embarrassing fact that he doesn't know another soul there, in which case it's kind to introduce him to your friend, too.

It shouldn't happen if your hosts do their job properly, but all too often they don't and it does. The man who was introduced to you when you arrived drifts off to talk to someone else. There you are stranded in a room full of strangers. The best solution is to find another woman in similar straits, go up and introduce yourself to her.

WHEN TO LEAVE

When the party begins to thin out, unless you're an intimate friend. A tired hostess doesn't welcome a comparative stranger left on her hands to the bitter end. If on the other hand you leave early, you may start a general exodus and break up the party. You should say goodbye to your host and hostess and thank your hostess. Many guests telephone the next day also to repeat their thanks, aware that giving even a small party without help entails an enormous amount of hard work.

Going to a Reception

Usually an official occasion, this is a grand version of the cocktail party, with someone in livery at the door to tell you where to put your coats, waiters to bring round the drinks and elaborate and expensive canapés. Very little introducing is done by the hosts except between 'Very Important People'. Others are left to seek out old friends or to talk to the people they brought with them. It's not usual to say goodbye to the host or hostess unless you've been specially invited by them. For wedding receptions, see pages 18–23.

THE RECEIVING LINE

This is a feature of receptions, banquets and large parties where the hosts could not otherwise manage to greet all the guests. Here is the form. Either husband or wife gives both names to the major-domo, 'Mr and Mrs John Smith'. If there is a daughter as well – 'Mr and Mrs John Smith and Miss Anne Smith'. In the case of a woman with an escort other than her husband the names are given separately. She gives hers as 'Miss Anne Smith', he gives his as 'Mr George Brown'.

When the major-domo calls your name out in a stentorian voice, that is your cue to walk in, shake hands with and say how-do-you-do to each person in the receiving line in turn, then pass on into the room. A wife always goes in in front of her husband.

Teenage Parties

Gone for ever are the romantic, parent-powerful days of frilly frocks and little dinner jackets, of shy girls and boys dancing decorously under the bright lights with mothers watching approvingly. Today's teenagers choose their own clothes and run their own parties – often not at all decorous – and only the bravest of parents dare to look in once or twice during the evening. The girls wear long skirts or trousers, the boys colourful separates – not a suit or a tie in sight. The room is in near darkness lit only by candles or the odd red or blue bulb, for the good reason that girls and boys spend most of the evening necking – practised teenage-party-goers pick their partners early in the evening because once he (she) has vanished into a dark corner with someone else there is precious little chance of getting him (her) back. Basic requirements for a party: a discotheque, preferably borrowed, a room with furniture moved out and carpets rolled up; and half a dozen bottles of cider, wine or beer – guests are usually asked to bring a bottle. Those rich enough to bring spirits have a selfish but sensible habit of hanging on to the bottle themselves for their own and their partners' consumption. Some hosts provide a bowl of punch. Invitations are usually by telephone and guests walk boldly up to each other and introduce themselves: 'I'm Mary Smith – who are you?'

Children's Birthday Parties

The average age of the guests is usually between two and seven, since after this age most children prefer birthday 'treats'. The six-to-sevens can be kept busy with treasure hunts (provided there are one or two children who can read the clues), but a younger age group means that the hostess has to work hard. It's a good idea to work out in advance a programme of simple games: 'pass the parcel'; 'dead lions'; 'statues'; 'oranges and lemons'; or whatever the favourite games in your locality are. 'Musical bumps' followed by tea gets the party off to a good start. A friend should be roped in to help if possible – to comfort little ones who suddenly burst into tears and want to go home, to stop the boys ganging up on the girls, and generally look after the children while you prepare the tea and dole out the prizes. At least some of the games should be non-competitive, as very small children can't bear being beaten. Older boys, on the other hand, may have to be bribed with the promise of a prize to join any organized games at all. If you can afford him, a professional entertainer is worth every penny.

THE TIME

Four to six PM is usual, two hours being about as long as any Mum on the receiving end can stand. Parents of little guests are expected to bring and fetch their children only, not to hang around unless specially asked to do so.

PRESENTS

The loot is an important feature. Each guest brings a present –
usually something very inexpensive, unless the children's parents are close friends. Mums of those embarrassing toddlers
who have to be forced by brute strength to hand over the lovely
boat/ball/aeroplane to an expectant host can avoid this crisis by
buying a duplicate gift beforehand.

Ideally, the children's party hostess keeps a record of who
brought what so that she can thank the appropriate Mum when
she comes to collect; but in practice such perfection is rarely
attainable, all record of the giver having disappeared long before in a chaos of rumpled paper.

On leaving, each guest expects a balloon and an inexpensive
present. The well-organized hostess stands by the door and
doles out these as the small guests depart, so that no one gets
forgotten. The odd extra balloon, small present or left-over
slice of cake comes in handy to give to brothers and sisters who
may arrive hopefully with Mum to collect.

THE FOOD

How Mum decorates the cake is a status symbol among small
children. Boys like ships, forts and trains; girls, little houses.
Mother's aids are plenty of silver foil, chocolate buttons,
Smarties and a square cake tin. Appearance is more important
than flavour. Most popular supporting foods are: little coloured
and chocolate biscuits; crisps; Twiglets; small individual
cakes; orangeade or Ribena; ice cream and jelly, a few small
honey, Marmite and jam sandwiches. The children all sit round
a table with plenty of room left for adults to pass things to
them. After the birthday boy or girl has blown out the candles
everyone sings 'Happy birthday to you'.

CLOTHES

Few parents go to the expense of buying special party gear. Girls wear their best dress and a pretty pair of shoes; boys, simply something clean and tidy with perhaps a colourful shirt and tie. Alternatively, among boys, cowboy and Indian parties are popular – and, since most children already have these costumes, this type of fancy dress party involves no extra sewing for Mum.

INVITATIONS

The most trouble-saving kind are those that have a tear-off section for the reply. But any of the children's party invitations in the shops will do. Snobbery about invitation cards begins later!

THANK YOU'S

Well-brought-up children should say 'Thank you for having me' to their hostess when they leave.

Staying the Weekend

This can mean one of two things – and since it is extremely uncomfortable to feel you have outstayed your welcome, it is worth getting them clear. 'Come and spend the weekend' means, Come on Saturday in time for lunch or dinner – your hostess should indicate which – and leave after tea on Sunday, unless pressed to stay to the evening meal. If you're asked for a 'long weekend' that means you're expected to spend an extra night, arriving in time for dinner on Friday. If you're coming by train it's up to the hostess to indicate which one it will be convenient for her to meet.

WHAT TO TAKE

A basic wardrobe for a country weekend is a skirt you can walk in or tough trousers, sweater, coat, waterproof shoes, flat-heeled indoor shoes, high heels and a dress – or nice trousers. If you are staying in a grand household where people 'change' for dinner the dress should be an evening dress, otherwise take an ordinary day dress. Nightdress or pyjamas should be the kind you won't be ashamed to own if someone else makes your bed. Your hostess should let you know if she's laid on any special entertainment, such as a party or a visit to the races, that will require extra clothes.

Guests are expected to bring their own toothpaste, but not their own soap.

WHEN YOU ARRIVE

Your hostess should show you to your room and leave you there while you do any unpacking or tidying up. She should also tell you where the bathroom is. If there's a man in the house he should carry your cases up for you. When you are ready, you come down and join the rest of the gathering.

WHO GOES TO BED FIRST?

Unfortunately there is no hard and fast rule – with the result that you sometimes get the ridiculous situation where hostess and guest both sit wearily on and on after dinner, each thinking that it's polite to let the other one break up the party. The best solution seems to be for the hostess to make the move when she sees her guests looking tired.

BREAKFAST

If your hostess doesn't tell you what time breakfast is, you should ask, so that you'll know when to appear the next morning. Guests who turn up before breakfast may find their hostess desperately trying to get through last night's washing up and not a bit pleased to see them.

ENTERTAINMENT

If some entertainment is laid on, you are expected to fall in with it unless you are asked if you would rather do something

else. Guests often contribute to the entertainment themselves –
and give their host and hostess a rest – by offering to take them
out to lunch or dinner.

THE PERFECT GUEST ...

Makes his or her own bed and offers to help with the washing
up, but doesn't press if the offer is refused. (A guest who
doesn't know where anything goes can be more of a nuisance
than a help.)

Cleans the bath after using it.

Doesn't pinch what is obviously the host's chair in the sitting
room.

Is always on time for meals.

Doesn't talk all the time.

Folds up the Sunday papers after reading them.

Answers 'Yes' to the question 'Did you sleep well?', even
though the noise of the radiator made it a sleepless night.

Doesn't wander round the house prying into the rooms.

Doesn't ask for things that aren't offered; though there are
of course, exceptions, such as a glass of water, an aspirin for a
headache, or an extra blanket.

Doesn't leave muddy footmarks on a pale carpet.

Turns off any lights he's the last person to use when he goes
to bed; even millionaires have been known to object strongly
when a guest left a light on all night.

TELEPHONE CALLS

The perfect guest doesn't use the telephone without asking and
keeps both outgoing and ingoing calls to absolute essentials.
Should you offer to pay for a call? Not for a local one, but if you
have to make a trunk call, then it is tactful to offer to pay even
though your hostess probably won't let you. Alternatively you
can find out from the operator what the call costs and leave the
money by the telephone.

LEAVING

Strictly speaking you need only thank your hostess and simply say goodbye to your host, though many people thank them both. The stock reply of hostesses slightly embarrassed by a guest's thanks is, 'You must come again'. This is just a meaningless murmur of words; it doesn't mean 'invite yourself again any time you like'. The best reply is to smile sweetly or murmur, 'I'd love to', and make your escape.

What to do about your bed? Leave it with the bedclothes pulled back, to air. Or, to save your hostess work, take the sheets off and fold them ready for the laundry or washing machine.

As soon as possible after you get home you should write and thank your hostess.

CHAPTER 11

DRESS AND APPEARANCE

NEVER BEFORE has the clothes scene been so confusing. Twelve years ago a woman knew exactly what to wear when; there were day dresses and cocktail dresses and evening dresses, and town clothes and country clothes and office clothes. Now most of this has vanished. The old comfortable distinctions are no more. Now a girl can wear trousers in the office and shorts at a nightclub; she can breast the waves in velvet and wear a cotton nightdress at a dance; she can cover her midriff on the beach and bare it in a restaurant; she can wear jeans in town and black in the country. It is all very different and confusing. And to make things worse, what to wear when is further complicated by the district you live in, who your friends are and, most of all, your age; so that desperate people are led to say wildly, 'You can wear anything anywhere today'. But that is still not quite true. And since finding oneself dressed in the wrong thing at a social occasion can still spoil that occasion for all but the most confident of us, I have drawn a few general guidelines.

Hats

No longer necessary except on the most formal occasions; they are worn to Buckingham Palace garden parties and most people also wear them to church weddings. They are also worn at certain grand social events dealt with later in this chapter.

Gloves

Disappearing from the young social scene even faster than hats. Except on very cold days, the young rarely wear them on any occasion less formal than a royal garden party. Middle-aged

people, however, still wear them for weddings and the elderly
don't feel properly dressed without them in town. As with hats,
if they return to the young clothes scene they will be worn more
for reasons of fashion than of etiquette.

But there is one occasion when most young as well as older
women wear gloves – largely for self protection – that is when
they have to do a lot of shaking hands, if, for instance, they are
part of a receiving line at a reception.

For those – a dwindling minority – who still wear gloves at
dances or cocktail parties, the old rules still hold good. If someone offers you a drink, an olive or a cigarette, take the right-
hand glove off. Always take your gloves off when you sit down
to dinner. Put them on again or not, as you please or as the
occasion dictates, afterwards. Before shaking hands, men if
they're wearing gloves (unlikely today except in very cold
weather) are supposed to take the right one off but women can
keep theirs on.

Trousers

An accepted part of the social scene today, they can now be
worn with high heels (once considered a terrible sin) – with the
result that most women can find a pair of trousers to suit them.
They are no longer only for the young and slim. Trousers
appear on women of all ages at all but the most formal occasions. Evening versions turn up at dinner parties and dances,
and for smart day wear the trouser suit has become almost as
much a classic as its ancestress the 'coat-and-skirt'. But for
balls and banquets, for royal garden parties and the royal enclosure at Ascot, most women wear a dress; for weddings too,
even though the bride herself will probably go away from the
reception in a trouser suit.

Town and Country Clothes

The distinctions between them are fast disappearing; those
that remain are based more on common sense than on etiquette.

Obviously you can wear more elegant shoes on a pavement than in a muddy lane and if you like to surround yourself with horses and dogs you are better off in a colour that won't show the mud and the hairs. But away from the mud and the manure heap, you can today wear most of the things that used to be considered bad taste in the country; plain dark colours, false eyelashes, lots of make-up and high heels. Conversely, you can, without raising eyebrows, go up to London in the same pair of slacks you drove the children to school in, although your sheep-skin jacket which is wonderful for a windswept country walk will be unnecessarily bulky for a shopping expedition in Knightsbridge.

But women do still dress up if they are going somewhere special in London – to a smart restaurant for lunch, for instance.

Men, as usual, are more conservative than women; the majority still go up to London in dark suits.

Clothes for Parties

If the card states 'Decorations', men are expected to wear tails, and decorations if they've got any. Miniature decorations, but no neck decorations or stars, can be worn with a dinner jacket, but men who turn up like this will be in the minority.

'White tie' on an invitation card means men are expected to wear tails.

'White or black tie' means most men will wear tails but if anyone doesn't own them or feel like going to the expense of hiring them, he can get away with a dinner jacket.

'Evening dress' on an invitation card means that most men will turn up in dinner jackets though at less formal occasions some adventurous young men will almost certainly appear in an assortment of evening suits. 'Dress optional' means that men can wear either a dinner jacket or a dark lounge suit – though younger men again will interpret 'dress optional' more widely.

Women take their cue in dressing from what the men with

them are wearing. When a man wears white tie and tails, with or without decorations, women wear their grandest evening dress. If a man wears a dinner jacket, a woman can wear an evening dress or evening trousers, depending on the occasion and current fashions.

When a man wears a dark lounge suit to a party, a woman today can wear a short or a long dress, depending on the occasion, but she shouldn't wear anything too grand.

The golden rule, when there are no guiding words on the invitation card and you are in doubt as to what to wear, is to ask – your hostess if it's a private party, other people who are going, if it's an official occasion.

AT A DANCE

Official dances, dinners and evening receptions are still usually white tie occasions. But at most private dances now, most men wear dinner jackets. And at the local political-party dance or tennis club dance people often wear something much more informal.

At hunt balls of fashionable hunts non-members generally wear white tie and tails – the hunt evening dress is so glamorous that dinner jackets tend to look under-dressed – but even here some men are usually to be found wearing dinner jackets.

SCHOOL PRIZE-GIVING

At fee-paying schools parents tend to dress-up for this occasion at the end of the summer term – the men mainly in light lounge suits, the women mainly in pretty dresses or suits, high heels, tights and sometimes a hat.

GARDEN PARTIES

Traditional garden party wear is a festive hat, pretty, expensive-looking dress, high heels and gloves. But, with the exception of those given at Buckingham Palace, formal garden parties are now rare.

FORMAL COCKTAIL PARTIES

Formal wear for cocktail parties in the evening is dark lounge suits for men. For women the picture is more confusing. Those who have time to change put on something prettier or made of a more expensive material than they would normally wear by day. Those who have to come straight on from their jobs wear a smart daytime suit or dress. At most cocktail parties today there are both short and long dresses.

If the cocktail party is before lunch men still wear dark lounge suits, women smart suits or day dresses with or without a hat.

PRIVATE DINNER PARTIES
(for the over thirties)

Men wear dark lounge suits, women simple long dresses, or separates with a long skirt, or evening trouser outfits. But if invited to wear 'black tie' or 'change for dinner' men come in conventional black dinner jackets or velvet jackets.

PARTIES FOR THE YOUNG

What is actually worn varies according to the particular set, but the accent is on deliberate informality, particularly for the men. The very young wear separates without ties, often without jackets, but clean, colourful and dandified. For grander affairs, velvet evening suits and white suits are gaining in popularity. A velvet evening suit can now go anywhere a dinner jacket does as well as to some white tie occasions. Even when they do condescend to copy their elders and wear a dinner jacket, many younger men disdain the bow tie in favour of a decorative but open-necked shirt or, arriving at a dance in a tie, discard it half-way through the evening.

London in the Evening

AT AN EXPENSIVE RESTAURANT, NIGHT CLUB OR DISCOTHEQUE

Most men wear a dark suit, dinner jacket or velvet jacket, and most women a long dress. Those who prefer to be sartorially more adventurous should remember that these are conservative establishments (because clients like them that way) and that men who don't arrive complete with both a tie and a jacket may still be asked humiliatingly to leave. Restaurant and night club managers don't like scruffiness either. Women are expected to look 'smart' – trousers are acceptable but shorts are frowned upon.

AT THE THEATRE

For an ordinary night nobody dresses up specially unless they are going on somewhere afterwards. Even for first nights people no longer dress up as much as they used to. In the stalls and circle men in dinner jackets and women in evening clothes mingle with people in ordinary day dress. People sitting elsewhere wear day clothes.

FILM PREMIÈRES

Dinner jackets and evening dress or evening trouser outfits are usually worn in the circle, ordinary day clothes downstairs. For the Royal Film Performance tails and full evening dress are worn by people likely to be presented to Royalty. On other occasions when Royalty are present, people likely to be presented to them wear dinner jackets.

ROYAL OPERA HOUSE, COVENT GARDEN

On the rare occasions of State Galas, men wear white tie, tails and decorations, and women full evening dress. When Galas of a more regular nature (such as the two annual Benevolent Fund Galas) take place, the men wear black tie, the women long dresses.

Apart from these occasions, there is no House rule as to dress at all, although on the opening night of the season and opening nights of new productions evening dress is sometimes worn. On ordinary nights, there is normally a mixture of clothing, ranging from dinner jacket to tweed jacket for men and their equivalent for women, although the majority of patrons generally appear 'smartly' dressed.

On all occasions, there is no dress regulation at all for patrons in the amphitheatre.

GLYNDEBOURNE FESTIVAL OPERA

'Evening dress, formal or informal, is recommended', states the Festival's official brochure. For the men this means traditional black dinner suit, or white or coloured jacket, velvet suit etc, and for the women short or long evening dresses or evening trouser suits. Evening dress helps to create the festive atmosphere, although there are always some members of the audience, particularly overseas visitors, who wear day clothes. Those who intend to picnic outside in the garden rather than eat in the restaurant bring rugs and warm coats.

Clothes for Sports

AT THE RACES

Anything goes if you're sitting in cheap seats or no seats at all, though most older men tend to wear suits. But if you're in the best seats and don't happen to back a winner, a day at the races can be very expensive indeed and people come correspondingly smartly turned out, especially for the Classics. Women wear suits or tailored dress and coat outfits, hats and high-heeled shoes in summer, tweeds and furs (including fur hats) and medium-heeled shoes or leather boots in cold weather. For the National Hunt races younger women often wear trousers and fun furs; but practically every woman over the age of fifteen in the Members' Enclosure or Paddock still wears a hat. The smartest men wear light lounge suits in summer, tweeds in winter with trilby hats, smart sheepskin or fur-lined jackets or covert coats.

ROYAL ASCOT

This is the one race meeting of the year where the horses are less important than the clothes. For people in the Royal Enclosure (no longer confined to an exclusive social set), Ascot is still one of the fashion occasions of the year. For publicity seekers it is an excuse to sport enormous extraordinary hats, but for most women the note is more sober though no less expensive – a crisply tailored look: beautifully cut dress, coat and hat outfits, made or bought specially for the occasion. Young girls, however, come in their favourite of the moment: long flouncy dresses and large floppy hats.

In theory the best dresses are supposed to be kept for Gold Cup day on the Thursday. In fact it depends on the weather. Anyone who has spent a small fortune on a special outfit for Ascot isn't going to miss the opportunity to wear it just because the only sunny day happens to be a Friday. And as there are always a lot of photographers around on the opening day, Tuesday, women like to wear something sensational then, too.

Men wear grey toppers and morning dress and look twenty times as smart as any of the women.

Women in the Grandstand, Paddock and Tattersalls wear suits or dresses and coats, with hats, but not such expensive outfits, as they would buy for the Royal Enclosure. Men wear lounge suits.

THE DERBY SUMMER MEETING

On Derby Day men in the best seats wear grey toppers and morning dress and women come correspondingly smartly turned out. On all other days men wear lounge suits.

POINT TO POINTS

People come prepared for the weather to do its worst, in flat shoes or boots, camel hair, tweeds, raincoats, sheepskin coats and headscarves.

CAR RACING

The scene is very different from a horse race meeting. The garb to adopt is something in which a girl could, at a pinch, change a wheel. Nearly all the women wear trousers.

HENLEY REGATTA

In the enclosures women wear traditional garden party clothes, complete with elaborate hat and high heels. The over thirties wear short dresses, the young girls long, but both age groups wear large floppy hats. Men wear rowing blazers and caps if entitled to them, otherwise light lounge suits.

THE FOURTH OF JUNE AT ETON

Fashions are generally more tailored than for Henley. Women wear silk suits or beautifully cut linen ensembles with hats and high heels. Some of the young wear long dresses or trouser suits. Most men wear lounge suits.

LORD'S

For the university and Test matches, men wear lounge suits. Even at the Eton and Harrow match, *the* social event at Lord's, this is now becoming the general rule. Fewer and fewer men each year turn up in the traditional morning dress and topper.

RIDING

Riding clothes are a law unto themselves, but a law that has become much less rigid during the last few years, helped by the advent of machine washable nylon stretch jodhpurs and rubber boots which – for the many who can't afford leather boots – simulate them very well.

For hacking (which means simply riding as opposed to riding in the show ring or hunting field), formal wear for both men and women is: jodhpurs with either long (rubber) or short riding boots, tweed jacket, white shirt and sober tie. The right gloves to wear are string and sweaters are usually polo-neck. Except that they rarely wear long boots, children wear the same. Women and children wear jockey caps which, for safety's sake, should be firmly anchored by chin-strap or harness. Long hair should be tidied into a net. Men wear jockey caps or tweed caps. It is correct to carry a riding crop – usually plaited string. Hunting crops are used only for hunting.

Such is formal hacking wear. But in practice many people today wear very informal clothes – jeans, bright patterned shirts and an assortment of sweaters. And the wearing of this casual gear no longer indicates to the initiated – as it would have done a few years ago – that you don't know one end of a horse from the other.

HUNTING

People who don't hunt often enough for it to be worth while to invest in proper hunting clothes can wear tweed jacket, yellow, cream or fawn breeches, brown or black boots, stock or tie and a bowler hat. This is known by the unglamorous title of rat-catcher, and is nothing like so impervious to rain and wind as the really correct form of dress. Here it is:

For Male Members and Subscribers. Scarlet coat (no, you need not call it 'pink'), white breeches, top boots, stock and top hat. Or: black coat, white breeches and top boots, or non-white breeches and hunting boots, stock and top hat.

For Farmers. Black coat, white, yellow, cream or fawn breeches, top or hunting boots, stock, hunting cap or bowler, or rat-catcher.

For women. Blue or black coat, yellow, cream or fawn breeches, hunting boots, stock and bowler. Hunting caps are only correctly worn by Masters of Hounds – including retired masters – hunt servants and farmers, but an increasing number of women wear hunting caps rather than bowlers in the belief that hunting caps are more becoming. Women who are Masters of Hounds, of course, correctly wear a hunting cap.

When riding astride it is correct to wear spurs, 'dummy' with a short shank.

Children. They can wear anything they like so long as they look neat and tidy. Usually they wear tweed coat, jodhpurs, jodhpur boots, shirt, tie and hunting cap – for safety's sake a 'must'.

SAILING

Practical newcomer to the sailing scene is the wet-suit; popular alternative, the oilskin suit. Oiled wool sweaters help to keep the cold-blooded warm; and the best shoes have non-slip soles. But what people wear in the last resort depends on what kind of boat they are sailing. No pair of trousers is too old or inelegant and any old sweater will do if you're in a dinghy, but on larger boats people tend to be smarter.

At most fashionable sailing clubs men still change into shore-going rig, that is blue serge slacks or grey flannels and a reefer jacket or blazer. The owner of the boat – he is never called the skipper, as sometimes there is a paid skipper – wears black buttons, the crew wear brass buttons. (According to sailing etiquette, the owner always buys his crew a drink when they come ashore after a race.) Women dine and dance in a wide variety of casual garments including reefer jacket and white trousers, short dresses, trouser suits or long cotton skirts and blouses. At informal sailing clubs where there are no restrictions on men's clothes, they fling tradition to the winds and dine and dance in polo-neck sweaters and gay shirts without jackets.

SKI-ING

The proper ski-ing clothes – proofed trousers and ski-ing jacket and goggles or sun-glasses – are essential. You also need cap or ear pads to protect your ears from the cold, socks to wear inside your ski-boots, and ski-mitts. Ski-boots can be hired, and you can buy little foam pads which go inside your socks to stop your ankle-bones getting rubbed. It is a good idea to take also for out-of-doors a warm short coat and high boots, and for indoors – which is usually very hot – thin sweaters or shirts.

Most women dine and dance in slacks, glamorous après ski ones in the smart resorts, less dressy ones in the humbler resorts where you can, if you like, dance in ski pants, but it is more comfortable to have something to change into. Men dine and dance here in sweaters and shirts; it is unnecessary to take sports jacket or tie – the whole atmosphere is informal.

A dance dress may come in useful over Christmas and the New Year, otherwise the average tourist need not take a dress at all. If she's been invited to a grand ball at St Moritz, of course, it's another matter.

For people who like to be in the fashion, ski fashions change from season to season and it is as well to find out before going what's being currently worn. But it is not a good idea to wait and buy over there, since the range of clothes is bigger and the prices are generally cheaper in London. Ski-tan cream is cheaper here too.

Making-up in Public

Still unacceptable in mixed company. Lipstick, powder and general make-up should be applied in the cloakroom except where office conditions make this impossible. The same goes for hair combing.

Suppose you get an eyelash or a bit of dirt beneath a contact lens at a dinner party can you remove the lens? To non-contact-lens wearers the sight of a lens being removed might be repulsive, so it is probably best to excuse yourself and make for the nearest bedroom, cloakroom or bathroom.

Churches

In Roman Catholic countries and Greece foreigners are expected to treat the churches as churches and not to treat them merely as art galleries. Although women can now enter St Peter's in Rome bare-headed, they are not allowed in with bare arms, in trousers or mini-skirts; and men must wear jackets. Neither sex may wear shorts. Lesser churches, particularly in popular tourists resorts, are usually more lenient; men without jackets and women in mini-skirts are generally allowed in, but if you wear shorts you may still be turned away from the door.

CHAPTER 12

THE MEN IN A
WOMAN'S LIFE

WOMEN'S LIBERATION, equal pay for women, and the insurance companies are doing their best to kill the notion that women are the weaker sex which was the romantic idea behind much of the etiquette observed by the old-fashioned 'gentleman'. Protective consideration for women at all times was his motto. The 'perfect gentleman' today is a fast disappearing species and those lucky enough to come across him will usually discover his age to be over forty. Here are the signs by which to recognize the perfect gentleman if you do meet him.

He walks on the outside of the pavement when he's with a woman in the street because the inside of the pavement is the safest and most comfortable place, especially when cars are splashing past on a wet day.

He offers his chair to a woman when there are not enough seats to go round..

He stands up both when a woman enters and leaves a room. (Women are entitled to remain seated, but they shouldn't stick rigidly to this right; if everyone else is getting up, it looks more natural and more courteous if they get up too, particularly if the new arrivals include anyone very old or eminent.)

If a woman friend comes over to his table in a restaurant he abandons his meal and rises to his feet, unless she's considerate enough to say, 'Please don't get up.'

At the dinner table he pulls out the chair of the woman sitting next him before sitting down himself.

He offers to carry anything heavy for a woman.

He helps a woman on with her coat if he happens to be standing by when she's putting it on.

If a woman drops something he will pick it up for her.

He lights a woman's cigarette before his own. In a gathering including his wife, he lights the other women's cigarettes before hers. And if there is a box of matches handy, he lights a woman's cigarette whether he's smoking or not. Even though he's a non-smoker, he sometimes carries matches with him for this purpose.

At a party he looks after the needs of any woman he is talking to, getting her another drink, putting down her empty plate, finding an ashtray for her. If there is a buffet meal, he sees that she has something to eat before tucking in himself.

He opens a door for a woman and lets her go first, except when it's more convenient for her if he leads the way. She goes first into the foyer of a cinema or theatre but he goes first into the auditorium in order to find the seats and buy the programmes. She gets into a car, a bus or a train before him, but he gets out first in order to open the door, or, if necessary, help her to alight.

But in a chauffeur-driven car he gets out last, as the chauffeur will do the honours.

Such are the basic rules for the behaviour of the perfect gentleman.

Naturally, not even he can observe all the rules all the time. It just isn't practicable. Few men these days feel themselves bound to offer up their seat to a strange woman on a train or bus unless she's very old or obviously pregnant. A boss who rose to his feet every time his secretary came into the room would never get any work done. Any man who tried to follow the rules at a large party where women are constantly coming and going would be leaping to his feet all the time.

But the perfect gentleman will follow the rules when they are practicable – particularly on formal social occasions.

ETIQUETTE FOR YOUNGER MEN

Their manners to women are much more casual than their fathers'. A young man today will rarely open a car door for a girl his own age, pull out her chair in a restaurant or help her on with her coat – in the belief perhaps that since she is probably earning as much money as he is and will, according to statistics, almost certainly live longer, she can jolly well do a few small things for herself. Similarly, he is unlikely to get up from his chair when she comes into a room or to make a point of protectively walking on the outside of her on the pavement.

Oddly enough, however, even the most modern young man when taking out a very pretty girl tends to observe many of the good old-fashioned rules that distinguish the 'perfect gentleman', behaviour that tends to pay off since, except for the hippy and very women's lib. girls, most women do still very much appreciate the old-fashioned courtesies. Another time when a well-mannered young man still observes the rules is when he is with the older generation. Though he may treat his girl friend socially just like one of the boys, he will still get up when her mother comes into the room; he will help his girl friend's mother on with her coat, open the car door for her and so on.

Incidentally, it is worth noting that one reason why the 'perfect gentleman' is a fast-disappearing species is because women seem to have forgotten how to say thank you. If he holds a shop door open for her, or gives up his seat for her in the tube, a woman should say thank you, not just stick her nose in the air as though she has received no more than her due.

HAT ETIQUETTE

Apart from a bowler hat to keep the cold winds from a bald head in winter or a soft hat at smart horsy occasions in the country, few men today wear hats at all, but for a man who does wear a hat, there are certain rules.

The 'perfect gentleman' will: raise it if he meets a woman he knows in the street; raise it again on taking his leave; take it off when entering a lift where there are women (many men also remove their hats when going into a women's shop); take it off when entering a private house or flat and leave it in the hall.

'SIR'

The use of this form of address by young men to older men as a sign of deference has practically died out. It is still used of course in the forces; by certain employees to certain employers and by garage, shop and hotel staff to clients.

Clothes

The main story in men's clothes over the last twelve years concerns the death of the idea that colour or decoration was 'loud' and 'flashy' and the re-birth of the peacock which lurks inside every male. Today the man who wears nothing but white shirts in his leisure hours looks old-fashioned in the dull pejorative sense of the word. And while the over-forties confine their flirtation with colour to bright shirts, sweaters and brilliant ties, younger men can appear clad from neck to heel in the most startling shades without exciting anything but envy in the hearts of their elders. The only reason why *they* don't wear brighter clothes is that they simply don't dare.

The secondary story in men's clothes is the growing accent on informality. Men appear now on casual occasions without jackets – for Sunday morning drinks at a Chelsea pub, for instance. And younger men discard their ties at every opportunity.

Coloured shirts are worn even with dark City suits. But the suit itself, mostly single-breasted today, has changed little.

BUTTONHOLES

It's not 'done' to wear a flower with decorations. Otherwise buttonholes are simply a matter of personal taste. Before the

First World War they were fashionable on most formal occasions, but now they are rarely seen except at weddings, where the bridegroom, bride's father and the ushers usually wear a white flower.

WAISTCOATS

The bottom button should be left undone.

OUTSIDE BREAST POCKET

Pens and pencils should never be worn in the outside breast pocket. The formal thing to wear is a white handkerchief either pointed or straight; alternatively, with a tweed suit, a coloured silk handkerchief. But many younger men prefer to ignore this fashion and leave their pockets bare.

SHIRTSLEEVES

No longer the crime they were before men finally succumbed to the use of deodorants. The man who was afraid of seeming effeminate if he smelt of anything except pure masculine sweat really needed his jacket to stifle the fumes. Younger men now no longer think twice about spending a social evening in shirtsleeves. A jacket, however, remains part of formal wear and should be worn to any formal gathering.

DOUBLE-BREASTED JACKETS

All the buttons should be done up, never the inside ones only.

EVENING DRESS

Traditional wear is: a black dinner jacket (or white in summer), a soft white shirt with pique front, a black bow tie, black trousers with a single row of braid, black patent leather shoes without toecaps, black nylon socks. Modern variations on this outfit include frilled and embroidered shirts, coloured shirts and coloured bow ties. The bow tie today is usually velvet. The scarlet cummerbund, useful for holding up trousers and concealing bulges, is growing in popularity. A velvet jacket – in dark blue, burgundy or green – is often worn today instead of the conventional black dinner jacket, either with matching velvet trousers or with conventional black ones. Black velvet is sometimes used for the jacket or for a complete velvet evening suit.

White or pale green suits (not in velvet) are sometimes worn by the young to evening parties, though rarely to very formal occasions.

EVENING DRESS (TAILS)

Tails are worn with a white stiff shirt with white wing collar; white bow tie; white waistcoat – waistcoat edge should never show under sides of coat; black trousers with a double row of braid; black patent leather shoes without toecaps, black silk or nylon socks.

Alternatively, the velvet evening suit with coloured bow tie and coloured shirt can be worn by the young or daring at both 'white' and 'black tie' occasions. Popular colour-scheme is burgundy velvet suit with burgundy bow tie and yellow shirt.

MORNING DRESS

This consists of black morning coat, soft white shirt with a starched collar, grey waistcoat, black-stripes-on-a-grey-ground trousers, black shoes with plain toecaps, black socks. Alternatively, the morning coat may be grey with waistcoat and trousers made of the same material; a coloured shirt and tie is sometimes worn with this. At an important memorial service, waistcoat, tie, gloves and top hat should be black. For a festive occasion, the waistcoat and gloves can be grey or buff, the tie is usually grey silk or black with a quiet pattern.

At weddings few younger men bother with hats or gloves since these can only be worn anyway for a few moments outside the church.

Manners with the Boy Friend

WHO PAYS?

Traditionally the man always paid for the woman, a tradition based on the fact that he usually had more money. Now that this is no longer so often true, what happens? Every girl still expects to be paid for when she is taken out for the first time by a prospective boy friend. What happens after depends on relative incomes. Where the boy's income is much larger than the girl's – if he, for instance, is a builder and she a shop assistant – he will normally go on paying; where, as with students, each has about the same income, she will usually, in the course of a regular relationship, pay her share. The situation, however, where the boy is not a prospective boy friend but simply a friend is quite different. Then the girl pays for herself from the beginning. Complicated though all this sounds, most young men make it quite clear by the form of their invitation whether they expect to treat you.

If he says: 'Will you come out with me on Saturday?' 'Will you have dinner with me tomorrow night?' or 'I've got tickets for such and such a show, would you like to come?' it's plain sailing. He's asking you out and he expects to pay for everything, including any transport, programmes if he's taking you to the theatre and any drinks in the interval. The only time you will have to put your hand in your pocket is in the ladies' cloakroom.

But if he says, 'Let's go and have lunch' he will almost certainly expect you to pay for yourself.

GOING DUTCH

When should you hand over? Most men – even those who will ask quite blatantly for a contribution – still feel bashful about accepting money from a woman in public. The tactful time to pay up is in private; before or after the restaurant meal, not across the table; before or after the film, not in the queue.

A girl whose boy friend is among the gallant few who insist on paying every time is unwise to argue. Far better to pay him back by giving supper parties in her flat or bed-sitter, or buying theatre tickets and then asking him to come with her. Alternatively, of course, she can always knit him a sweater.

THE ENTERTAINMENT

If he's doing the paying, he chooses. He says, 'I thought we'd eat at such and such a place', and you're expected to trot meekly in his wake however much you loathe the restaurant of his choice. But it's just possible he may ask you where you would like to go. That may mean that money's no object with him, but far more often it means he's inexperienced in taking girls out and has not yet learned to avoid the pitfalls. If you answer honestly, you may let him in for far more than he can afford. A way out of the dilemma is either to give him a choice of restaurants at varying prices or simply to say what kind of food you fancy. 'I'd like to eat Chinese' leaves it open to him to take you to the most expensive Chinese restaurant in town or to the cheap one round the corner.

If on the other hand it's been settled that you will pay your share of the bill, you have an equal share in the choice of entertainment.

GOODNIGHTS

There you are, standing on the doorstep, totting up what the evening has cost him. It comes to half your week's salary. What does he expect in return? Girls about to live in London for the first time are usually informed – by some man, of course – that they will have to sleep with every man who takes them out. This, the bright ones discover, is not true; a girl is still entitled to do as she pleases. But if she doesn't want to sleep with him she should leave him on the doorstep, because if she invites him in he will expect more than a cup of coffee and a biscuit.

HOLIDAYS

Young men and girls go on holiday alone together today without provoking any special comment. It is no longer assumed that they will sleep together, and even if they do, your morals today are considered to be your own business at least as far as the world goes, though parents may have different ideas and insist on a foursome.

Man and girl usually share costs – the easiest way being to split all living expenses equally, regardless of whether her lobster costs more than his chicken or he has an aperitif and she doesn't before dinner.

But if either of them buys any clothes or presents to bring home, they pay for them out of their own money.

PUTTING OFF AN UNWANTED BOY FRIEND

If every time he rings up you say that you're busy for the next three weeks he should tumble to the fact that he's lost your interest. But if the boy friend is the type in whom hope springs eternal and you haven't the moral courage to tell him frankly you never want to go out with him again, the only way to get rid of him, and the way that will hurt his pride least, is to tell a white lie and say there is someone else.

CHASING A MAN

A woman who indicates a preference for a man before he has shown any special liking for her is now an accepted part of the social scene. Girls can now go up to a man at a party and introduce themselves; it's all part of the new equality of the sexes. But men are conventional creatures. They still prefer to think that the initiative is theirs. And it is still not done for a girl to ask a man out for a first date.

So what can you do if you meet a man you fancy at a party and he doesn't ring up to ask you out? You can invite him among a group of other people to supper, drinks or coffee. But after that it's up to him again.

Manners with your husband

Though even the most model husband doesn't follow all the rules of gallantry with his wife at home – he can't be expected to jump up every time she comes into their sitting room – in public he should treat his wife just as courteously as he does other women. His behaviour should never indicate that he shares the view implied in the old music hall joke: 'Who's that lady over there?' 'That's no lady, that's my wife.'

But it's not only husbands who may be at fault. How many wives interrupt their husbands' funny stories with, 'Oh Jack, you've missed the point again', or, 'That's not how it happened at all'! Husband and wife should work as a team, helping, not belittling each other and, on the surface at least, their relations should appear harmonious. The old rule about not washing dirty linen in public still holds good. However much husband and wife may long with the aid of an audience to prove once and for all how utterly unreasonable the other one is, this is embarrassing for other people.

HOW TO REFER TO YOUR HUSBAND

By his christian name to friends. As 'my husband' to people who don't know his christian name. You are supposed to refer to him as 'Mr Smith' or 'Sir John' only when talking to someone on a much lower social level, and even then 'my husband' is becoming more usual today. But 'Mr Smith' or 'Sir John' is the formal way to refer to someone else's husband; 'your husband' is informal.

A similar rule obtains for men when speaking of their own and other people's wives.

MAKING UP A FOURSOME

The convention is for husbands and wives to split up. In the car, for instance, you sit next to the other woman's husband and vice versa unless, of course, there's too little room in the back seat for this to be practicable.

CHAPTER 13

HIGH LIFE

Royal Etiquette

SHOULD YOU accidentally call the Queen Mother 'Love' or
'Dearie' when she comes to visit your council house garden, no
one is going to worry – but it is more comfortable to know what
you are expected to call her. Over and above ordinary good
manners, there are certain conventions of behaviour observed
with members of the royal family and nobody else. Of course,
how far you observe these traditional formalities must depend
on circumstances. If you find yourself on a ski-ing holiday or at
a dance with one of the younger members of the royal family
you would not behave in the same way as you would if you
were presented to the Queen or the Queen Mother on an
official occasion. But it's worth noting that those most often in
touch with the Queen err on the side of observing, rather than
omitting the formalities. The following details have been
checked with Buckingham Palace.

INTRODUCTIONS

People are always introduced to Royalty – the correct word is
presented – never the other way round. The form is: 'Your
Majesty (or Your Royal Highness) may I present Mr Jones',
or: 'May I present Mr Jones, Ma'am (or Sir),' Ma'am is pronounced as spelt, not, as popularly supposed, 'Marm'. (It is
a colloquial shortening for 'Madam' and is written in full.)

TALKING TO ROYALTY

When should you address members of the royal family as 'Your
Majesty' or 'Your Royal Highness' and when can you use the

less formal 'Ma'am' or 'Sir'? Servants use 'Your Majesty' or 'Your Royal Highness' all the time. For everyone else the form is, in the first instance, 'Your Majesty' or 'Your Royal Highness' followed by 'Ma'am' or 'Sir'. What you should never do is to address them directly by name as 'Prince Philip' or 'Princess Margaret'.

When asking a question of a member of the royal family it is more formal to use 'Your Majesty' or 'Your Royal Highness' than 'you'. 'What does Your Majesty think of the new exhibition at the Tate?' 'Would Your Royal Highness like me to', etc. But obviously, if you were asking a string of questions, it would sound unbearably pompous if you used 'Your Majesty' or 'Your Royal Highness' in every sentence.

REFERRING TO MEMBERS OF THE ROYAL FAMILY IN THE PRESENCE OF ANOTHER MEMBER OF THE ROYAL FAMILY

Formally, personal pronouns such as 'he', 'her', 'they', etc., are avoided, also 'husband', 'sister', 'mother', 'daughter', etc. They are referred to either by name, 'The Queen', 'Prince Philip', 'Princess Margaret', by people on a similar social level, or as 'Her Majesty', 'His Royal Highness', 'Her Royal Highness', by servants, unless, of course, there was likely to be some confusion as to who was meant.

It is a fallacy that 'you shouldn't speak to Royalty until they have spoken to you'. If you see the Queen in the street or at a party it is not good manners to go up and speak to her out of the blue. But if you are presented, there is no reason why you shouldn't speak before she does if there is an opportunity. (Usually the person doing the presenting will give the Queen a lead: '... Mr Smith, who has been our foreman for the last twenty years', in which case it would be natural for her to speak first.) Similarly there is no reason why you shouldn't start a new topic of conversation. The Queen would probably welcome it – as usually the onus of keeping the conversation going falls on her.

WRITING TO ROYALTY

The formal way to begin a letter is: 'Your Majesty' or 'Your Royal Highness'. But people on a similar social level who have met the person they are writing to begin simply, 'Madam' to the Queen and to other female members of the royal family, 'Sir' to male members of the royal family. Among the many equally correct ways to end a letter this is a very usual form: 'I have the honour to be, Your Majesty's (or Your Royal Highness's) most humble and obedient servant.'

As in talking, personal pronouns such as 'you', or 'he' and 'her' when they refer to another member of the royal family, are generally avoided; Your Majesty, Your Royal Highness, Princess Margaret or Her Royal Highness, etc, being used instead, as in the following excerpt from a letter written by the late Earl Attlee to King George VI:

> 10 Downing Street,
> March 2nd, 1949
>
> ... Mr Churchill made the same suggestion which Your Majesty made yesterday, as to the possibility of Your Majesty being the President of India. ...

But when this convention would result in a string of 'Your Majesties' or 'His Royal Highnesses' many people would lighten the sentence by substituting the occasional personal pronoun.

WHEN SHOULD YOU CURTSEY?

At the beginning and end of each meeting with the royal family. If you were presented, you would curtsey; if the Queen visited your home you would curtsey when you greeted her and when you said goodbye to her; if you had an interview with her, you would curtsey on entering and on leaving the room. If you were staying in the same house party as a member of the royal family, it would be polite to curtsey the first time you saw them in the morning and when you said goodnight. It would also be good manners to curtsey if you happened to see the Queen in a shop and she caught your eye or smiled at you. (Members of the Queen's household curtsey if they meet her in one of Buckingham Palace's passages.) At a royal garden party, when the Queen comes out of the palace, guests form a long lane. The Queen passes down it and guests bow or curtsey as she draws level with them.

HOW TO ADDRESS THE ENVELOPE

The following are the correct styles of address:

Her Majesty, The Queen
Her Majesty, Queen Elizabeth, The Queen Mother
HRH The Duke of Edinburgh
HRH The Prince of Wales
HRH The Princess Anne
HRH The Princess Margaret, Countess of Snowdon
HRH The Duchess of Gloucester
HRH The Duchess of Kent
HRH Princess Alexandra, The Hon. Mrs Angus Ogilvy

All children of the Sovereign, whichever generation they belong to, get 'The' after HRH. But when a prince is also a duke (Prince Charles excepted), envelopes are addressed: HRH The Duke of —.

As a general rule you should add either all honours and decorations or none, but in the case of the Duke of Edinburgh, he has so many that usually KG, KT only are put after his name, except on very formal documents.

WHAT TO WEAR AT A ROYAL GARDEN PARTY

The conventional dress is morning coats for men, wedding-type clothes for women. But the Queen has made it known that she does not expect people to go to expense they cannot afford to buy or hire special clothes; and at least twenty per cent of the men at a royal garden party do wear lounge suits – this twenty per cent has, in the past, included Lord Snowdon. Women's clothes can be any colour they like.

HATS AND GLOVES

Hats and gloves are normally worn to a daytime function when one of the royal family is present. But this is simply because these functions are formal occasions and hats and gloves are part of formal wear. When the Queen goes to horse trials or to watch polo other people come bare-headed, in headscarves or however they please. Gloves are not worn at the semi-informal dinner parties given by the Queen at Buckingham Palace.

AT A DANCE

Even in royal circles white tie and tails are becoming a rarity. At Buckingham Palace today they are worn only on the most formal occasions, such as state banquets for visiting heads of state. Dinner jackets are now worn for nearly all receptions and dances given by the Queen and the Duke of Edinburgh.

Can a man ask a member of the royal family to dance? Not unless he's been presented to her. If he has, it is probably expressly so that he should dance with her. The polite form is: 'Ma'am, may I have the honour of this dance?'

Whether you can politely leave a party before a royal guest depends on the size of the party. At a small one it would be good manners to wait for them to leave, but if there were several hundred people no one would notice if you simply drifted off.

DINNER WITH A MEMBER OF THE ROYAL FAMILY

The royal lady, as the most important female guest, sits on the right of the host, the royal gentleman on the right of the hostess. (As regards going into the dining room, it's worth noting that at semi-informal dinner parties at Buckingham Palace, the Queen and Prince Philip follow the normal procedure, the Queen going into the dining room with the women guests first, followed by Prince Philip and the men guests.) But on a formal occasion where people go in two by two, the Queen goes first with her host, followed by Prince Philip and the hostess.

Etiquette for Debutantes

In spite of the social revolution that has taken place over the last twenty years, in spite of the fact that Buckingham Palace set its seal on it by bringing deb's presentation parties to an end, debutantes are still with us. Indoor servants have disappeared from all but the most stately homes but every year about two hundred girls officially still come out. Of these, about fifty or sixty only, it is true, do the full season, at a cost of between £5,000 and £10,000. The other girls take the season casually, attending only a few of the star events and parties and spending the rest of the time getting on with a career. But the disadvantage of this is that a girl who doesn't go in for the full social round will almost certainly find herself a wallflower at the dances she does go to where everyone except her will know everyone else.

For the deb who does the full season even a secretarial course may become too exacting. She may have as many as seven dances in the week, four cocktail parties, two tea parties and two lunch parties.

For the three months from Queen Charlotte's charity ball in May to Goodwood Races in July, which mark the end of the London social season, she will lead a life of parties, pretty clothes and boy friends – of lunch parties, tea parties, cocktail parties and dances ending at 5.30 in the morning. And in September the socializing will start again with dances and shooting weekends in Scotland, followed by more dances and parties in London.

It is in fact a concentrated course in getting to know the 'best people' – at every party she will meet the same set and from it she will probably eventually choose her husband.

Not that it would be fair to suggest that this is the whole purpose of giving your daughter a season. For a deb who is pretty and not too shy, the season is a fairytale interlude between school and settling down to the humdrum of everyday existence. It is also an opportunity to make friendships which may last a lifetime.

But invitations don't just arrive out of the blue. In order to get invited to all the parties, a deb has to meet more of her fellow debs than she will already know through going to an expensive school. This entails a good deal of preliminary organization on her mother's part, all beginning with a series of lists. There is a list of debutantes, a list of party dates, and a list of desirable young men. The pattern is then as follows:

MUMS' LUNCH PARTIES

Though the eventual object of the exercise may be a husband, the season is organized by women for women, and the whole merry-go-round is set in motion by a series of hen parties.

First, the Mums' lunches. The deb's mother invites six or eight other debs' Mums. Each of her guests will invite her back to lunch, when she will meet still more debs' Mums.

More informal than they used to be, these lunches now take place in a London home rather than in one of the expensive hotels or exclusive clubs, and a favourite topic of conversation is the list of eligible young men. Which boy should and which should not remain on the list? As a result of these sessions many a young man's social life has been abruptly curtailed. 'On very poor evidence,' complains a current deb, 'because the mothers never really know what goes on.'

DEBS' TEA PARTIES

Once organized by the Mums, these are now organized by the girls themselves. They send out postcards to their selected guests among the other debs:

Caroline Smith and Amanda Jenkins are giving a tea party

at 300 Redcliffe Road, Monday, March 3rd, at 4.30. Do hope
you can come.   RSVP

Through a succession of these parties a large number of girls
soon know each other. The tea parties usually have some gim-
mick; one deb gave an 'ice-cream party', another a 'milk
party'. Alternatively a deb can give a lunch party in some 'in'
place. The heyday of the debs' tea parties is from March to
May though they do go on throughout the season. The debs
wear jeans unless a Mum is present when they feel they should
dress more respectably.

The favourite dates for London dances are July and September when plenty of young Oxbridge men are available;
country dances take place at weekends. The usual starting time
is between 10 and 10.30, although there is no need to get there
until an hour or so later. Supper – cold salmon, chicken in
aspic, strawberries and cream – is served at about 12.30. Other
features include elaborate room decorations, a band that plays
on into the small hours, and a discotheque.

The main drink is champagne but orange juice and coffee
are laid on for the debs, few of whom appreciate more than the
odd glass of alcohol.

Invitations are sent out about eight weeks before the dance
and should be engraved – with a reply card attached, in the
case of country dances, asking guests if they would like to be
included in a house party.

DINNER PARTIES

It is one of the conventions of the season that on the night of a
dance all the debs who have been invited must also be asked to
dinner parties beforehand. The dance hostess has to see that
they are. Usually she asks other debs' Mums – and tells them
which girls to invite.

For very large dinner parties, formal cards are sometimes
sent, but invitations are more often by letter:

Dear Miss Montgomery-Smythe,

I am giving a dinner party at — on — for Lady Bracknell (or 'for Amanda Bracknell's dance') and I should be delighted if you could come.

Miss Montgomery-Smythe writes back:

Dear Lady Blank,

I should love to come to your dinner party on Saturday, May 28th.

The dance hostess herself gives a dinner party, generally in the hotel where the dance is to take place, including her daughter's closest friends and any notabilities among the guests.

AT THE DANCE

The dinner party guests and their hostess arrive at roughly the same time, but from this point on the old conventions are thrown to the wind. No longer do the young men automatically wait downstairs while the girls leave their coats in the cloakroom – today it's every deb's delight for himself. And the same goes for the deb. No longer does she feel bound dutifully to dance with at least four or five men including those she sat next at dinner. Now she may dance the night away with just one man.

COUNTRY DANCES

Increasingly fashionable in recent years, the country coming-out dance has its snags. Because so many weary guests driving back to London at 5.30 in the morning have been hurt in road accidents, they are now customarily put up for the night. And this means more work for the deb's mother. She may be lucky enough to live near other debs' Mums, in which case they will probably invite the young people to stay on for the entire weekend. But debs' Mums are but thinly scattered round the countryside – there are rarely enough to provide beds for some two hundred guests – and many a country vicar's wife has found herself inviting, putting up and giving a dinner party for six complete strangers whom she will never see again. What is more, she will have to manage all this with the help of only her daily woman and possibly, if she's lucky, a couple of kind-hearted assistants from the village.

THANK-YOU LETTERS

A debutante is expected to write to her dance hostess, e.g.:

Dear Lady So-and-So,
   I did so enjoy the dance. The flowers looked lovely – the colour scheme was so original – and the band was marvellous. In fact, everything combined to make it a fantastic evening. I loved every moment of it.

A debutante is also supposed to write a thank-you letter to her house party hostess. And many girls, but not all, write to their dinner party hostess as well, e.g.:

Dear Mrs Blank,
   It was so kind of you to have me to dinner and such a super one too. It made a wonderful start to a wonderful evening.
   I hope you enjoyed the dance as much as I did.

It is not, however, considered necessary to write and thank for a cocktail party, which many debs' parents now give instead of a dance.

THE DEB'S WARDROBE

After her dance this is one of the most costly items. A deb can't very well manage with less than twelve evening dresses – including three grand ones, one white for Queen Charlotte's, one for her own dance and one for other balls. Then she will need something special to wear for Royal Ascot, and she will probably need something too for the Eton and Harrow match at Lord's, the Fourth of June at Eton, Henley Regatta and Goodwood Races, Cowes and Glyndebourne. She will need clothes for cocktail parties and expensive discotheques and for first nights at theatres where she will sit in the most expensive seats. Then she will need clothes for country weekends and shooting parties and, if she's lucky, clothes for the South of France where a popular deb will get invited during the summer. Although the season officially comes to an end in July, deb dances and parties start up again after the summer holidays and continue until Christmas.

INDEX

Constance Spry
Rosemary Hume

THE CONSTANCE SPRY COOKERY
BOOK (illus)   £1.25

'Cooking is a combination of science, art, invention, and a few other things.' Constance
Spry and Rosemary Hume, founders of the
Cordon Bleu Cookery School, share the secrets
of a lifetime of experience, covering all aspects
of cooking and entertaining, to make life easier
both for the novice cook and for the normally
competent hostess in a tight spot. An imaginative mine of information and inspiration for
the bored housewife. A must for every home.
'This fat, full, delectable opus could easily
prove the favourite wedding present. The
range is extraordinary. The book is admirably
bound and printed, and contains good photographs.' – SUNDAY TIMES

Craft Books

JEWELLERY   95p

Thomas Gentille, jeweller and instructor, presents a unique introduction to the art of jewellery making in this handsome, fully illustrated book. Easy to follow, step-by-step instructions guide the beginner through ten stimulating projects, including rings, pins, cuff links, earrings, pendants and combs. Mr Gentille, whose jewellery has appeared in many exhibitions, also introduces and explains the techniques of casting, forging, enamelling, granulation and electroforming.

WEAVING   95p

In this exciting, fully illustrated book, the world of weaving is opened to the beginner. Step-by-step instructions introduce the novice to the frame and four harness looms. The dyeing of yarns, using both commercial and natural dyes, is explored. A Rya rug, poncho, place mats, bags, a tapestry, pillows and stoles are among the projects that Miss Znamierowski has designed for the beginner to create.

Marianne Kohler

THE SECRETS OF RELAXATION
(illus)   40p

True relaxation is the key to the release of
mental and physical strain. Marianne Kohler's
many different techniques to achieve it, from
the simplest stretching exercises to the luxur-
ious Japanese bath, bring both lasting and
immediate benefits. As well as the lesser known
exotic approaches to relaxation, Miss Kohler
presents the age-old methods of yoga and
meditation that pave the way to the individual's mastery over his emotions and bring
both bodily health and inner peace.

These and other PAN Books are obtainable
from all booksellers and newsagents. If you
have any difficulty please send purchase price
plus 7p postage to PO Box 11, Falmouth,
Cornwall.
While every effort is made to keep prices low,
it is sometimes necessary to increase prices at
short notice. PAN Books reserve the right to
show new retail prices on covers which may
differ from those advertised in the text or
elsewhere.